THE SUNNY SIDE OF THE ALPS
From Scotland to Slovenia on a Shoestring
Living in Slovenia (Book One)

ROY CLARK

Dedication

Dedicated to the good-hearted and gracious people of the Scottish Highlands and the Alpine region of Slovenia.

Contents

Chapter 1 Seizing the Day

'Hey, how do you fancy being spanked on top of a mountain on your next summer holiday?' I asked Justi as we walked up the long, narrow lane in the cold and wet of a Highland winter's day.

'What are you on about?' she asked, sounding disgruntled yet perhaps a little intrigued (OK, the intrigue bit was just my wishful thinking) as we braced ourselves against another gust of sleet-filled headwind.

'I read a great article in the paper today about Slovenia and about climbing its highest mountain—Triglav. Apparently, people who reach the summit for the first time are light-heartedly whipped on the bum with a piece of rope,' I explained. 'It sounds a great country,' I babbled on. 'Mountains, lakes, seaside and sun. We could cycle there in our walking boots and do Triglav. I could even put a bit of rope in my pannier just in case,' I added hopefully.

In another twenty minutes or so, we'd reached Birchwood, the old foresters' house we rented on the edge of a pine forest, a large plantation below the majestic group of hills known as the Grey Corries that rise above the villages of Spean Bridge and Roybridge in the Scottish Highlands.

The house was quite remote, being part of an old hunting estate with the 'big house' and its stalkers' cottages being our nearest neighbours. There was no double glazing or any sign of efficient insulation, so damp was a problem, but we loved it with its wonderful seclusion amid the spectacular Highland landscape.

One day, not long after we'd first moved in, Justi said, looking out of the window, 'I wonder if these two are going to be our first visitors?'

An elderly couple, probably in their 80s, were standing by the gate, the man looking thoughtfully at the house.

I went outside and asked if I could help them in any way. The old man expressed his thanks and said that he didn't need any help; he and his wife had just come 'for a last look' at the house. He explained that he'd lived in the house when he was a child, before his father's task of finding work had led them to a life in the city. He reminisced that he and his brother had shared one of the two bedrooms at the back of the house that looked out onto the vegetable garden and the kennels that used to house the stalkers' dogs.

'Please come in and have some tea,' I offered, eager to hear more about his time living in the house, but he politely declined and said they'd have to be on their way. As they headed towards their car, he turned for one last look at the house and recalled how his older brother, aged about ten, had etched his signature onto one of the bedroom window panes.

As soon as I was back indoors, I raced upstairs to look at the old sash windows in our bedroom, and sure enough, in the bottom right corner was a spidery signature scratched into the glass. I wanted the old man and his wife to know, but I'd already heard their car moving off down the gravel road. I now knew that the old sash windows that rattled in their frames every time the east wind roared down the glen were at least 70 years old.

Justi and I shared the chores of making the fire, brewing a pot of tea and feeding Bryn, our ever-patient, ever-hungry border collie. I was eager to show Justi the newspaper article about Slovenia and persuade her that it would be the best cycling/camping/walking holiday in the history of cycling/camping/walking holidays. Embellishing descriptions with prompts, gasps and dramatic pauses, I read the text that told of emerald-coloured rivers, flower-filled alpine meadows, majestic mountains and friendly locals.

At the time, the Slovene tourist board were trying hard to promote the country using the catchphrase 'Slovenia—the Sunny Side of the Alps' and, having experienced a succession of particularly wet Scottish summers, Justi was soon nibbling at the bait.

'The Julian Alps, not as high as the French or Swiss Alps. No glaciers, huts everywhere with food and blankets, no need to carry loads of kit and with better weather—imagine that!' I added with an approving and suitably pleading stare at Justi before directing my gaze (and hopefully hers) towards the rain-thrashed windows.

'Well, it does sound good,' agreed Justi, 'but we won't have enough holiday time to cycle all the way there and back. We'll only have three weeks max.'

'No problem, I've already thought about that,' I chipped in. 'We could use the European bike bus like we did this August and get dropped off on their furthest eastern route, somewhere in Italy maybe, and cycle from there. Slovenia has a border with Italy,' I added, trying to sound knowledgeable, though I'd only Googled that a few hours previously.

We'd already enjoyed several cycle/camping holidays in France, Italy and Switzerland. We'd found cycle touring to be the best way to really experience a country as it was possible to cover a fair distance but still enjoy a close connection with the land you pass through that isn't possible in a car. Living so far north, we made the best use of our limited holiday time by using the European Bike Express, known simply and affectionately to many British cyclists as the bike bus, to get us into mainland Europe. This coach company uses large bike trailers and runs from the North of England, with various pick-up points throughout the UK and drop-off points on the continent. Back in 2001, they offered three routes for UK cyclists to escape the great British summers and help dry out their sodden Lycra.

So, with the plan of an exciting summer adventure starting to coalesce in our heads, our attention turned to getting on with our lives through another Highland winter. The area we lived in, Lochaber, was usually a busy place in the summer months, and rightly so. Tourists, walkers and climbers would flock in to view or climb Ben Nevis, Scotland's highest summit, while others would drive the scenic road to the Isle of Skye or take the steam train to Mallaig.

The nearby town of Fort William would bustle with people spending their cash in the tartan wool and outdoor shops or, as was more often the case, sit in the cafés and bars staring out at the rain, recounting their midge hell experiences to anyone who'd listen.

In the winter, the tourists had mostly gone. The midges, the tiny biting insects that are the plague of the Highland summer, had definitively gone, and the locals would party as only highlanders can. Parties were usually impromptu. One minute you'd be sitting down with a book for the evening, and the next, you'd be on your way to a local house party with the three folk who stopped by with a wee can or ten.

The following day was usually one of mortified regret if the evening had progressed as far as taxis to McTavish's club in Fort William, something I'd done occasionally during the early days of my first six Highland years before Justi had arrived. Organised ceilidhs in local village halls were common through the winter months and gave a chance for the locals to let their hair down and enjoy themselves without having to help tourists struggle through a Gay Gordons reel. It seemed that a good number of Highland folk are talented musicians, and more than once we'd been left speechless by incredible fiddle or pipe solos being performed by some local school kid.

The best part of the winter, though, was on those rare blue-sky days when the ground was frozen hard and a glistening white coat of snow draped the mountains. Walking and ice climbing in the Scottish mountains on such days was one of the reasons I'd left my home city of Liverpool and made a life in the Highlands. The incredible raw beauty and peaceful solitude of the Highlands had also led Justi there, and it didn't occur to either of us at that time that we'd even consider leaving.

However, as the winter progressed, it became more obvious by the day that Justi was no longer happy in her work. She was a qualified speech and language therapist, and along with three others, her job involved visits to schools and private individuals in an area that covered over 5,000 square kilometres. She was acutely aware that the service was stretched beyond its functional limit and that the quality and future of the profession appeared to be in decline. There was never enough time to supply the real help and service to all the individuals she was contracted to work with. The emotional stress of having to deal with heartbreaking cases of autism and kids with severe learning and physical disabilities was also beginning to wear her down. She'd been working for over seventeen years as a professional in her field, and she now found herself dreaming of a change, of doing something new.

By late January 2002, she confided that she couldn't see herself continuing to work as a speech therapist beyond the end of that year. The bad run of wet summers and heavy grey skies had also contributed to her need for a change, and she started to talk about job options that would see us moving abroad to live. She looked into the prospect of teaching English as a foreign language and soon began a course to gain a qualification. She'd already been doing an Open University diploma course in French for the last three years, and so we started to think about the possibilities of moving to France. We were both Francophiles and had enjoyed cycling and skiing holidays there in the five years since we'd met.

It would be a serious life change for Justi; she would be giving up her career and starting anew in a completely different field. It was a lot less of a commitment for me as I didn't have a professional career. I viewed the prospect of moving to France as merely an exciting adventure.

I'd had many jobs in the Highlands. My background was in catering, so for the first three years, I'd been a cook before moving on to work in outdoor shops, food deliveries, forestry work and gardening. I'd also worked as a ski-lift operator, stacked shelves in a supermarket, worked behind a bar, and had even been a part-time postman for a while. I'd enjoyed all my jobs, but that was perhaps because they'd never made me feel tied down. I'd been drawn to the Highlands and its breathtaking landscape, and a job, any job, was just a necessary part of my being able to live among its mountains and glens.

In essence, it was the same for Justi as she'd also been drawn there because of her love of the hills. Before she'd arrived in Lochaber, she'd lived and worked as a speech therapist in North Wales close to the Snowdonia National Park and had served as a member of the Ogwen Valley Mountain Rescue Team. While living in Wales, she'd also enjoyed many trips on the Holyhead ferry to visit Ireland, the country of her grandparents. The wild landscapes of Ireland's west coast had even prompted her to consider applying for a job on the Emerald Isle before she finally decided to come to Scotland.

For me, a day in the office could involve skiing down the steep corrie headwall to reach the 'Braveheart' chairlift station, planting trees in a remote Highland glen, or delivering fish and game to country house hotels located in idyllic locations on the Isle of Skye. But for Justi, it meant either long hours in the car driving to a remote school and home visits, or tedious administration work under bright fluorescent lighting in the clinic office. It went without saying that wherever we'd end up next, it would surely involve mountains.

In retrospect, I think the first stirrings of Justi's 'winter of discontent' had started the previous autumn. In September of 2001, we'd turned 40 within ten days of each other and enjoyed a humdinger of a party at our house, with both local friends and a good number from Liverpool and Wales.

At 4 a.m., after we'd finished loading the dishwasher with the final round of glasses, Justi and I poured a last tot of whisky each and took a seat at the kitchen table, away from the snoring bodies strewn about in our living room. We giggled like drunken 40-year-olds as a cacophony of snoring and peculiar intestinal noises drifted through from the living room. We both agreed what an excellent party it had been and then, after a thoughtful pause, Justi asked, 'What now?'

'How do you mean?'

'Well, can you see us being here for the next five years?' she asked. 'Turning 40 feels like a bit of a turning point. I'm happy here, but I don't want to be looking out of the same office window until I retire.'

A sad incident the previous year had also made us both think deeply about seizing the day when opportunities come along. Robert, one of my cycling friends, had suggested that he and I go to France to take part in l'Étape du Tour—a one-day event in July for amateur cyclists to ride a stage of the Tour de France. That year, the millennial *étape* (stage) involved a 154-kilometre hilly stage in Provence that finished on the summit of the renowned Mont Ventoux. I didn't need much persuasion, and within a few days, we'd booked our places on the starting list for the 2000 Étape du Tour.

We started doing a few training rides together, talking excitedly about the upcoming event and noting how our fitness increased with each outing on the bikes. Then Robert started to miss planned rides, explaining how his workload had increased and that it left him with little spare time. I understood this and knew he was also committed to his young family, but I was confident we'd still be doing the event together.

One of our later training rides started at our house in Spean Bridge and finished on the top of the Bealach na Bà, a narrow pass on the Applecross Peninsula. As we wobbled carefully off, struggling along the gravel lane on our narrow-tyred racing bikes, Justi chuckled as she snapped a photo of us. Robert was a big guy, and as I was only half his size, we looked an unlikely 'little and large' pair in our identical cycling club shirts.

It was the best ride we could plot to mirror the actual étape route, being 150 kilometres in distance. It was a lovely day, and we rode through stunning scenery, but as we began the final ascent up the steep pass, Robert began to cramp up. I suspected it was caused by his missing a few training rides as I felt fine, and Robert was always a much stronger rider than me. In true Robert style, he battled on to the top before getting off his bike to give his calf muscles a rub, but he gave no cause for concern about doing the planned event.

About three weeks before we were due to leave for Provence, Robert contacted me to explain that his boss needed him to work during the time of the étape. He sounded forlorn, and I knew he was genuinely gutted by this turn of events, but he hoped that next year would be different. I was very sorry too, but I was also determined to make the most of the opportunity and do the ride. I didn't have the same commitments as Robert; we didn't have children or a mortgage to worry about. I explained the situation to Justi, and we managed to turn the event into our summer holiday that year.

Tragically, in early September, Robert was killed in a motorcycle accident; there wouldn't be a next year for him. His death contributed to our attitude and belief that seizing the day and being open to opportunities and new experiences was something that Justi and I valued and that we still believe in to this day.

Chapter 2 Slovenia Calling

Our Slovene holiday plans were put on the back burner as Justi's search for employment took priority. She regularly checked the *Guardian* overseas job section for an advert that would, hopefully, read something like, 'English language teacher wanted for small school in the French Alps. Attractive job package to include cosy chalet with gingham curtains and window boxes full of geraniums. No experience necessary. PS. Applicants who can bring a handyman/gardener with them will be given preference.'

There wasn't much doing in the dream-job section, and it began to look like our whole idea might be a fantasy with no substance after all. Our initial, upbeat enthusiasm in searching and discussing the job ads each day slowly began to wane.

Then, one evening in late February, when we were out walking Bryn along the lane, I casually asked Justi if she'd seen anything of interest.

'Um, well, there was one that sounded a bit interesting,' she replied, 'but it's not in France. It's in Slovenia.'

'Slovenia!' I immediately recalled our forgotten holiday plans as all the images of sunshine, snow-capped mountains and flower-filled meadows that the article had spoken of suddenly popped into my mind again. 'What does it say? Do you think you could do it? Do you have the right qualifications?' I fired at her, not giving her any time to answer between shots.

'What about France?' she asked, sounding exasperated at my unbridled enthusiasm.

'France, yes, of course. I'm sorry. I forgot for a moment,' I said, realising I wasn't being very understanding or very persuasive. 'I'm sure your French will never be wasted. I mean, we could still go on holiday to France in the future,' I added, failing spectacularly to rein in my Slovene prepossession.

'Let's get home first, and then we'll have a proper look at the job advert,' Justi said resignedly.

I was anxious to get back to the house as soon as possible to pursue the Slovene cause. We arrived back, and I put the kettle on and lit the fire while Justi booted up the computer. She printed out a copy of the advert from the jobs section and brought it into the kitchen. She sat down at the kitchen table as I brought two mugs of tea over.

'Right,' she said. 'The Slovene Ministry of Education is looking for a qualified person to start work as an English language assistant in the state school system this September. "The applicants must be native English speakers and have a degree and a TEFL (teaching English as a foreign language) qualification. Furnished accommodation will be provided for the successful applicant."'

Speaking Slovene wasn't a requirement. Justi had two degrees and was a native speaker but, although she was expecting to have all her TEFL coursework finished by August, she wouldn't have the actual qualification until October. However, she was confident she would get it, and so was I—she's as bright as a button.

'Great!' I enthused. 'What are you waiting for? Let's download the application form and…'

'Hang on, hang on!' said Justi. 'What about France? I've put three years of time and effort into learning French.' Her unwillingness to show any enthusiasm for working in Slovenia was understandable. She'd worked long into the evenings on her French course and had been to two summer schools in France. She'd also set her heart on the possibility of finding work and making a home there and believed it could constitute the next chapter of our lives.

Over the next few days, Justi gradually came around to the idea of applying for the job. I turned up the dial on the persuasion offensive and talked up the Slovene cause by drawing her attention to articles and information I'd found on the internet. Back then, the web was strung a little thinner than it is today, with limited information, so most of what I found was from the Slovene tourist board and holiday companies, and naturally, they were all singing the country's praises.

I also pointed out that France didn't seem to need (or want) any English TEFL teachers, and that she hadn't had any replies from the letters she'd sent to language schools in various hilly regions. By the end of the following week, her application form, along with medical and police checks, had been posted off to the British Council (the intermediary for the Slovene Ministry of Education) in the capital city, Ljubljana.

After about two weeks, an email arrived informing us that her application had been received and that a telephone interview would be arranged the following week if Justi was still interested.

'Wow, that's brilliant!' I exclaimed as ridiculous, fanciful images of me herding cows with Bryn on a high alpine pasture while Justi taught English to kids sitting on benches outside a sun-warmed chalet burst into my mind. Although still filled with uncertainty, Justi admitted that she was also feeling pleased about being accepted for the interview and had started finding out more about Slovenia.

The telephone interview was arranged to take place the following Friday at 6:30 a.m. UK time, 7:30 a.m. European time.

'Blimey, that's a bit early,' I muttered as we read the email, not knowing then that most Slovene businesses, and even schools, start at 7 a.m.

On Friday morning, I was up at 5:30 to light the fire and make a brew, feeling quite nervous on Justi's behalf. She wasn't nervous at all about the interview; she just felt very odd to be going to an interview wearing her dressing gown.

We sipped our tea as the fire slowly warmed the room. It was still pitch dark outside, and we heard an owl hooting in the tall birch trees at the end of the garden.

At exactly 6.30, the telephone rang, and Justi picked it up.

'Hi,' said a friendly female voice. 'My name's Dana. Am I speaking to Justi?'

I stood up quietly and walked through to the kitchen to avoid causing any distraction, though I left the door slightly ajar so that I would be able to gauge how it was going. Justi sounded happy and relaxed, and from what I could tell from the muffled yet cordial-sounding tones of Dana, the interview seemed to be going well. After about fifteen minutes, I could sense that it was winding up and that Dana was now taking questions. I heard Justi say that, should she be successful, I would be coming to Slovenia with her, and would that fit in with the accommodation package offered?

There was a pause then some muffled answers that I couldn't quite make out.

'I'll be bringing my dog too. Is that OK?'

Dana had explained to Justi that, although it would be OK for me to come, we must be aware that the salary offered only equated to about 50% of an equivalent UK assistant teacher's, and I wouldn't be allowed to do any work without a permit as Slovenia wasn't yet a member of the EU. She said bringing Bryn shouldn't be an issue, provided suitable accommodation could be found by the school.

Over breakfast, Justi sounded upbeat. 'That seemed to go well,' she enthused, 'and Dana sounded very fair and efficient, yet quite laid back too.'

'Well, that's a good sign. I mean, Slovenia must be a great place to work, eh?' I said with equal enthusiasm.

'We'll just have to wait and see now,' she replied, trying to sound indifferent in an attempt to reel me in. But it was too late as she'd already confirmed it was a good interview, and she felt quite confident that they would offer her the job. They would inform her of the outcome within the next week. With that, we went back to bed for an hour and wondered if we'd ever have to get used to Slovene working hours.

Chapter 3 Getting to Know You

While we waited to hear if Justi had got the job, we broadened our quest for information about Slovenia. We picked up a copy of the Slovenia *Lonely Planet* guide, thinking we could still use it for our planned cycling holiday if Justi weren't accepted for the teaching position. Our combined knowledge of the country was very sketchy, and most of what we knew we had only learned in the past few weeks.

Some twenty years earlier, I'd spent about ten hours in the country on a day excursion while on a camping holiday near Venice. My hazy memories included a ferry crossing and coach trip to see a performance of the beautiful white Lipizzaner horses somewhere in the south of the country, followed by a visit to the impressive Postojna cave system a bit further north.

The only other things I could recall (probably somewhat distorted by time) were an unmade road and two unshaven, gun-toting policemen languishing menacingly against their patrol vehicle. It was a bit of a whirlwind tour at a time when Slovenia was still very much part of communist Yugoslavia.

So far, reading our new guidebook, we'd discovered that Slovenia is a small Central European republic surrounded by countries whose names we were more familiar with—Italy, Austria, Croatia and Hungary. It also has a short stretch of coastline on the Adriatic Sea, squeezed between Trieste in Italy and the border with Croatia.

Slovenia became an independent republic in 1991 after dramatically breaking free from the Federal Republic of Yugoslavia. Because of this, Slovenia had no part in the terrible Balkan Wars that followed the break-up of the communist state.

The country had been occupied throughout its entire history, and notable invaders included the Romans, Attila the Hun, the Ottoman Turks, Napoleon and Hitler. As we read between the lines of history, it seemed to us that, on the whole, the Slovenes were a peaceful people, rooted in their land. They were people who had waited patiently to govern their own country for hundreds of years until, in 1991, their first real chance for lasting independence came along. That's not to say they didn't try to repel the invaders over the years—memorials to WW2 partisan resistance fighters are widespread throughout the country and give testament to their brave struggle. But being such a small country, located right in the middle of Europe and encircled by bigger neighbours, they were unable to resist the imperialistic forces that had always surrounded them.

With a land area about half the size of Switzerland, Slovenia is a relatively tiny country. However, with its population being just over two million (and about 15% of them living in Ljubljana), it didn't exactly sound crowded. This was important to us as we both loved the space and solitude that was there in the Highlands whenever we needed it.

The language was a Slavic one, and to us, it looked scarily incomprehensible. There didn't appear to be any of the word similarities that are found in the Germanic or Romance tongues, which at least allow the luxury of an educated guess. The Slovenes had developed their own 'dual' version too—there is a single (one thing), dual (two things) and plural (three or more things) form to every noun, with a different word ending for each. They also apparently had lots of dialects. Oh dear... It didn't sound as though learning the lingo would be an easy task, although we agreed we wouldn't be put off from trying should we find ourselves living there.

We diligently soaked up all the historical data, but the things that inspired and excited us the most were the descriptions and images of the landscape. We were impressed to read that over 50% of the land is forested, and about 90% is higher than 300 metres.

The Julian Alps sounded like a larger, sun-warmed version of the Cuillin mountains on the Isle of Skye, the UK's most 'alpine' mountain range, being magnificently steep and looking impregnable. Slovenia's Soča River is apparently one of the most pristine rivers in the whole of Europe. Pictures of the incredible emerald-green water had to be Photoshopped, we thought; surely no river could be both so crystal clear and so vibrantly colourful?

Chocolate-box pictures of Lake Bled, with its tiny island and castle atop a vertical crag backed by a stunning panorama of hills, also fired up our longing to see Slovenia for real.

The Slovenes themselves were described as a people rooted in their traditions and culture yet very modern and forward-thinking with regard to politics and business. They were also portrayed as being very hospitable, helpful and honest.

Justi and I had both enjoyed sampling the cuisine of different countries on our cycling tours, and Slovenia's menu sounded like it had a lot to offer a pair of foodies. We weren't big meat eaters, so it was concerning to read that the Slovenians were. However, there also seemed to be mouth-watering alternatives at hand like savoury dumplings made with cheese and flavoured with herbs, and risottos made with wild mushrooms. The Slovene cakes, desserts and wines also sounded wonderful—the two most popular traditional cakes included savoury ingredients like cottage cheese, poppy seeds and tarragon that appealed to a pair of covert, sweet-toothed calorie watchers.

Last but not least on our Slovenia fact-finding mission was its climate, and this was perhaps of a little more interest to Justi than it was to me. Because I worked outdoors year-round in all weathers, I'd become quite tolerant of the rainy days, of which there were many in the Highlands. I'd even built up a resistance to that plague of western Scotland's summertime—the midge.

I didn't notice the bad weather days as much as Justi because, when the Highlands enjoyed a spell of sunshine, I was outside working. Justi, on the other hand, was usually working indoors, and there had been so many weekends when she was off work but it had rained heavily and plans to walk hills or go cycling together were scuppered.

For such a tiny country, it seemed unimaginable to us that Slovenia could have three distinctly different geographical climates, but this is how it is. A continental climate in the east, a sub-Mediterranean one at the coast and an alpine climate in the high mountainous areas that gives warm summers and cold, snowy winters—this last, of course, was the one we were most interested in.

After absorbing all this information, I remember enthusiastically telling a mate from Liverpool how it was possible in Slovenia to go alpine skiing in the morning then have a meal at a seaside restaurant in the afternoon.

'Yer what?' he said. 'You'd look a bit of an idiot wearing yer ski boots at the seaside.'

Chapter 4 Good luck in Slovakia!

The email from the British Council had arrived. It said that Justi could start work at the beginning of October and that they'd let her know by the end of the following month where in the country and in which school she would be placed.

We looked at each other for a moment, trying to gauge our emotions and response as the news sank in. We were in a mild state of shock, but smiles broke out on our faces, and we did a silly little jig around the kitchen table, clinging onto each other by the shoulders. Bryn sat up and watched us with a slightly worried expression then curled up again in his basket looking resigned—he was well used to the bizarre behaviour of his human pack mates by now.

The implications of moving to another country unleashed a myriad of questions that raced around in our minds demanding immediate answers, but we regained some sense of responsible adult behaviour, and I opted to make dinner while Justi took Bryn out for a short walk.

When we regrouped over dinner, we chatted excitedly, recalling our reactions and how we'd felt when we first read the email. With our initial excitement starting to subside, we slowly turned our attention to some of the most critical issues we now faced: telling friends and family, giving up our jobs, and organising all our worldly goods—what to take, what to sell, and what to leave behind in case it didn't work out and we decided to come back.

Justi phoned her mother and broke the news to her.

'Slovakia, that sounds an awfully long way away. Isn't it next door to Russia?'

'No, Mum, Slo-veen-eea,' said Justi with a little more stress on the syllables. 'It's next door to Italy.'

Justi's mum, Betty, took the news in her stride; she was, after all, used to her daughter's relatively unconventional lifestyle when it came to moving and choice of pastimes. At the end of the conservation, Betty told Justi she was pleased for us both, and she would go and look for Slovakia in her big world atlas.

'No, Slo-veen-eea!' said Justi into the phone, but Betty had hung up and was probably already heading towards her bookcase.

My parents sounded mystified when I phoned them.

'Slovenia used to be part of Yugoslavia, Dad,' I explained. 'It's very scenic, lots of mountains.'

'But what will you do out there, and what about Bryn?'

'Don't worry, Dad. I'm sure I'll find some work too, and Bryn will be fine. We're taking him with us, of course.'

They were concerned, not least about Bryn, whom they adored. They always enjoyed looking after our easy-going collie when we left him with them at the caravan they owned in the Yorkshire Dales, during our annual summer cycling holiday.

'And how are you going to get to Slovakia?'

'It's Slovenia, Dad, and I imagine we'll drive there.'

'Hi, Roy, your dad says something about you and Justi going to Slovakia,' my mum said as she took the phone.

'No, Mum, he means Slovenia; we're going to Slovenia,' I said, frustrated about the confusion and wondering about my ability to convey the name of our chosen destination.

This confusion about Slovenia and Slovakia continued as we told more family and friends about our intended move. Slovakia had the advantage in the 'recognisable name' category, probably because of its word association with Czechoslovakia. Until relatively recent times, Slovenia wasn't very well known to UK citizens, who had never really considered the various amalgamations of the south Slavic regions but instead had registered Yugoslavia as a single country.

Maybe Slovakia just rolled off the tongue a bit easier too, but for whatever reason, it certainly wasn't just our friends and family who got them confused. In 1999, the then US President George Bush Jr. mixed them up spectacularly, and so did Italy's prime minister, Silvio Berlusconi, who introduced the Slovene prime minister, Anton Rop, as the prime minister of Slovakia at a news conference in Rome— even though Slovenia is Italy's next-door neighbour.

Even recently, during the autumn of 2017, I received a text message from a friend who said I must be feeling proud because a Slovene professional cyclist had just won the World Road Race

Championship for the third time. Not knowing who he meant, I Googled it to discover that Peter Sagan from Slovakia was the winner.

We decided we would aim to leave Scotland by mid- to late-August and drive down to Southport and Liverpool to spend a couple of weeks with our families before we left for Slovenia. We also wanted to take a trip to North Wales to say goodbye to friends. The main drive to Slovenia would be our summer camping holiday, so we devised a scenic route that would include a week or so in France. This gave us just over four months, which seemed plenty of time, to sort out all the necessary tasks of moving that lay ahead.

Before we'd met, Justi and I had both moved house many times, but the last move had been one we'd made together. We'd lived in one of the old stalkers' cottages for about a year before moving just 250 metres up the gravel road to take up residency at Birchwood. The cottage we left had been difficult to heat and was very dark inside, being north-facing, so we'd jumped at the opportunity when Birchwood had come up for rent because it had more space, was a bit more airy and had a garden. We were still at a point in our lives when 'damp and draughty' didn't take precedence over 'wow, what a view'. It still doesn't, if we're honest. We'd both become very attached to the house, so it was difficult to contemplate leaving.

We informed the estate office of our notice and Ted, the factor,[1] soon visited us. We knew that he'd recently accepted a position on another estate and this might be the last time that we'd see him. He seemed genuinely sad that he was losing us as tenants as we hadn't given him any cause for concern in the five years or so that we'd been renting the house. Occasionally, we'd badgered him for tins of paint for decorating, and he'd always considered our requests. Any agreement made was a fair one, or the 'best he could do', in his words.

We arranged that the keys would be handed to Ted's replacement at the estate office in Fort William when the time came, and he asked us where we were going. He raised his eyebrows in interest when we told him.

'Ah, Slovenia, very nice,' he said confidently, as though he knew the country well, before striding off in his crisply ironed shirt and smart tweed jacket, his green wellington boots crunching on the

[1] The person who manages a Scottish estate.

gravel.

It seemed that a good number of estate officers had a military background and, therefore, a good knowledge of European life beyond the Highlands. I suspected that he at least knew the difference between Slovenia and Slovakia.

*****

For the last three years, I'd been working as a self-employed gardener in our local area after I'd become fed up with having to travel increasingly long distances for my forest contract work. Justi had persuaded me to write an advert on a postcard offering my services as a gardener and pin it on the village notice board. I was sceptical at first, but after two weeks, just when I'd started to think that no one in the village needed any help with their gardens, the phone rang. It was Mrs Macleod, the colonel's wife, and she needed her croquet lawn mowing before the weekend.

'All the equipment is here for garden work. My husband will show you where it is when you arrive.'

'Great, thank you, Mrs Macleod. I'll be up in twenty minutes.'

Feeling pleased that I'd just reinvented myself as a gardener, my confidence took a tumble when the colonel presented me with an immaculate lawn in front of their lovely house. The crochet hoops in the centre stood like matchstick-men figures, and I imagined they could see through my pathetic bluff: 'You're not are a real gardener, are you? You've never even seen a real crochet hoop before, have you? You're just a cocksure Scouser out of your depth, aren't you?' they sneered.

I was unsure where to start. The grass didn't exactly look like it needed anything more than an orderly trim, and was I supposed to remove the crochet hoops, and should I mow the lawn in neat lines or circles?

Somehow, though, I must have done something right as the next day, I got a phone call from Mrs Cameron, another lady of means and a friend of Mrs Macleod. Word of mouth is how life in the Highlands operates, and within about three weeks, I had enough regular garden work to make a basic living. I worked in tiny gardens, grand gardens and some that looked like wild meadows. Sometimes, my clients asked me to do jobs not related to gardening at all, like collecting their shopping, decorating their houses (perfect on a rainy day!) or even, on occasion, burying their deceased pets.

I regretfully went about my task of informing them that I'd no longer be able to work for them after mid-August. I'd enjoyed my time as a Highland gardener and hoped that I'd be able to pick up where I'd left off should our Slovene adventure not work out well.

Justi had found that, before handing in her notice, she'd struggled with worry and doubt about leaving the service and ultimately her career; she became quite stressed about the whole prospect. Well-meaning friends and colleagues questioned her wisdom in giving up her career and pension for a job that paid only half the salary in an ex-communist country she'd never even been to. Justi looked at life another way; she was much more worried that she would end up doing a job she no longer enjoyed for another twenty years.

Happily, though, once she'd handed her notice in, she felt as though a huge weight had been lifted from her shoulders, and she felt free as a bird that had just sprung its cage door. She was now able to look forward to a new chapter of her life that didn't seem as tightly scripted as the one she was leaving. It seemed this new path could lead anywhere—hopefully to sun-kissed mountains.

Over the next few weeks, we cleared space on the study floor and started to make three piles—one for the things we hoped to sell at car boot sales, one for things we wanted to take with us, and one for things we would leave behind with family and friends who had offered space in their attics and sheds.

The crooked towers of different-sized boxes soon started to outgrow the study, and before long, the hall also looked like a disorderly warehouse. The wobbling, car-boot tower blocks had achieved sufficient height and mass to warrant a search in the classifieds to find where the next sale would be. We were in luck—it was to be held just outside Fort Augustus, a village at the southern end of Loch Ness, about a 40-minute drive away.

After an early breakfast, we loaded the car with all the things we could bear to part with, which included a battered old biscuit tin, the type with a cheesy-looking portrait of an angelic child dressed in Victorian style clothes on the lid, which Justi placed in last.

'Why are you putting that in? We've already got a tin to put change in; it's on the dashboard.'

'You never know; someone might like to buy it,' replied Justi, sensing that I was about to question her choice of things to sell.

'What? No chance! No one will buy that. I'd be embarrassed trying to give it away,' I said, closing the rear hatch with an extra-hard, dismissive thump to make my point. It was the first car boot sale that either of us had been to, and it probably showed as the organisers tried to redirect us back into the correct field after I'd driven up a parallel track to a cowshed. Everyone else seemed to know exactly where they were going and what they were doing as they parked their cars and vans in neatly spaced lines then deftly produced impressive displays of what was, mostly, tat.

I turned the engine off and said, 'Right, let's get the pasting table out then,' but before I had time to open the door, a lady knocked on my window, asking questions while pointing and gesturing to something in the back of the car. I wound the window down.

'How much will you be wanting for the wee biscuit tin?' she asked.

'Ten pence, please,' said Justi as she got out of the car to fish the tin out of the back. The lady was delighted with her rusty tin, and the smug smile on Justi's face taunted me for the rest of the day. She's never let me forget it, and now I always think twice before I question her judgement on anything.

By midday, most sellers had begun packing away their leftover goods, and the sale was effectively over. We'd made about £70. Not bad, we thought, for a morning's work that had mostly involved drinking tea and chatting to the locals. Throughout the summer, we went to another four car boot sales and made a similar amount at each, all of which we saved towards our planned move.

As the pile of things to sell slowly diminished, the pile of things to take increased. They included skis, a bike each, camping equipment, books, summer and winter clothes, Bryn's basket, my guitar and Justi's saxophone. At some point just before leaving, the computer tower, monitor and speakers would also be added. There was also a box of old cameras and a heavy ancient metal tripod I'd acquired as I'd taken up photography with fanaticism. Feeling encouraged that I'd recently sold a number of my photos to a local craft shop, I was hoping to continue with my camera craze in Slovenia.

This list was by no means exhaustive, and we soon realised that our Ford Escort saloon wasn't the best vehicle for shifting two people, their dog and their worldly goods across Europe, so we began searching for a used combi-type van. They were obviously popular; not many appeared in the second-hand section, and the ones that did were well outside our price range.

As our leaving date drew ever nearer, I felt concerned that we wouldn't find the right vehicle in time while viewing yet another high-mileage rust bucket that looked as though its owner had used it to house his hens. Feeling at a bit of a loss, I mentioned our combi conundrum to a friend, whose opinion on all things mechanical I respected and valued. He immediately suggested I'd been looking at the wrong type of vehicle and recommended that I should look out for a good estate car instead.

'There are more available; they're better priced, and they can pack a lot of stuff. I used to use one for my painting business,' he said, adding that insurance costs would probably be a bit less too. His straightforward words of wisdom and experience switched a light on in my head.

'Thanks, Brian. I'll go and check some out,' I said, putting the phone down and eagerly starting a new search through the Scottish *Automart* magazine.

A Renault Savannah caught my eye. It was in our price range, had 65,000 miles on the clock, and it looked big. Its name sounded big.

I phoned the owner, who lived in Aberdeen, and quizzed him about the car's condition. He responded with all the right noises, so we arranged to meet at his business, located in a small industrial estate on the outskirts of the city.

The white Renault Savannah was parked outside the grey roller doors of a small business unit, and the owner, expecting us, appeared with the keys. We chatted briefly, and I explained why we needed an estate car, stressing mechanical reliability as the priority. Showing us a pile of service receipts, he assured us that it had been well looked after as he'd used it for his work.

He opened the rear hatch, and we peered into the interior. It was vast! With the rear seats lying flat, an enormous wasteland stretched to the far-off escarpment of the front seats. I saw a train of camels in the distance while a few tumbleweeds rolled past us and blew across the industrial park. Renault had named their car well.

After a short test drive, we handed over the agreed £1,000, and as Justi drove ahead in the Escort, the ex-owner waved me on my way, shouting, 'Send us a postcard from Slovakia when you get there!'

Chapter 5 Leaving the Highlands

Justi received another email from the British Council informing her that the Slovene Ministry of Education had assigned her to a school placement in a spa town in the east of the country. She went to search the web to find the exact location while I fetched our *Lonely Planet* guide. We both recognised the name of the place, Podpetek, from the evenings we'd spent at the computer and reading books during our Slovene fact-finding missions.

The internet and guidebook confirmed the basic knowledge we had on its location and the fact that the town had a square surrounded by very grand-looking, classical buildings. It was one of the many spa towns in the east of Slovenia, a country which has a thriving industry of healing waters. They're used not only for rest and recuperation but also by the medical system for convalescence and complementary therapies.

The town was just a few kilometres from the Croatian border, set amid hilly countryside that supported a mixture of small-scale farming, vineyards planted on impossibly steep slopes and attractive forests of what appeared to be mostly deciduous trees.

Situated in the east, it was as about as far away as possible from the Julian Alps that had sparked our interest in visiting the country, so our initial response to the email was one of slight disappointment. However, the area looked beautiful, and although it lacked any rugged alpine grandeur, there were a couple of bigger hills close to the town that looked as though they'd give a good day's walk, one being just above 900 metres in height and one just under. We also reasoned that, as it's such a small country, we'd easily be able to nip over to the Julian Alps during weekends and holidays.

Another email soon followed, this one coming directly from the school, informing us that an apartment had been found in one of the beautiful neoclassical buildings on the corner of the old square. The owner had confirmed that pets were allowed.

'Wow, brilliant! Does that mean I'll be allowed in too?' I quizzed Justi.

'Only if you're well behaved and don't get up on the furniture.'

All the pieces of our planned move seemed to be coming together.

'Why don't we invite friends round for a leaving meal?' I suggested to Justi. 'We could try and do something with a Slovene theme.'

'Good idea,' she replied, 'but you're on your own when it comes to choosing and cooking anything Slovene I'm afraid. I'm still too busy with my final course assignment and winding up my speech therapy work in the evenings.'

'OK, I'll search the web for Slovene recipes and come up with something.'

One recipe immediately caught my eye—venison goulash. I noticed it because I'd recently been doing some gardening for our neighbour, Dougie Campbell, who was the local gamekeeper. I'd refused to accept any payment for my work as I knew he always kept an eye on our house whenever we were away. We both liked Dougie and felt that just knowing him had enriched our lives more than any amount of money could.

As far as we knew, Dougie had worked for the estate all his life, and he seemed quite ageless—he could have been anywhere between 50 and 70 years old. He was a gamekeeper in the traditional mould, wearing the typical stalker's outfit: a tweed jacket, shirt and tie and wellington boots. He also wore an ancient tweed cap which he'd doff to ladies and always remove before entering the house. He refused to change the hour on his watch for British Summer Time, saying that his work started when he got up and finished when he got home.

One day, not long after Justi had arrived in Scotland and moved into one of the stalkers' cottages, there was a knock at the door. She opened it to see Dougie standing there, wellington boots cleaned and his cap held politely in his hand.

'Are you going out in the hills today?' he asked.

'Yes, probably. Why?'

'Well, if you see any Hillwalkers,' (Dougie always pronounced Hillwalkers somehow with a capital H) 'tell them to be careful. We're stalking today, and they disturb the deer. Remember, I've got a gun and a licence to kill.'

Not yet aware of Dougie's wry sense of Highland humour, Justi was shocked for a moment, but the playful glint in Dougie's eye told her neither she nor the wayward Hillwalkers had anything to fear.

I'd remembered how Dougie had offered me some venison as payment when I'd refused cash for cutting his lawn. As we weren't big meat eaters, I'd politely declined, but now I thought it would be an excellent opportunity to see if the offer was still on the table.

Dougie was pleased when I asked, and later that evening, I heard his Land Rover pull up outside on the drive. I went out to greet him, and he handed over a haunch of fresh venison. He produced a hip flask of whisky from his jacket pocket, and we passed it back and forth while we chatted. He thanked me for the garden work I'd done for him over the last year and wished us well on our new venture. I'm not sure if Dougie knew or cared where Slovenia was, and as for travelling, he'd told me he'd 'been as far as Glasgow some years ago.' He was deeply rooted and completely at ease in his surroundings—except when 'the Hillwalkers' were about.

Thanks to Dougie, I managed to concoct a passable venison goulash for our friends, but as a way of combining adventures to come and adventures past, we washed it down with a bottle of Highland single malt.

*****

One of the most difficult tasks leading up to our departure was getting all the necessary documents from the vet to make sure that Bryn could come with us to Slovenia. He had more pieces of paper than Justi and me combined. In 2002, it was still early days in the European pet passport scheme, and as Slovenia wasn't yet a member of the EU, it meant two different levels of bureaucracy had to be satisfied. The previous week, we'd taken Bryn to the vet, and he was now the unwitting owner of a passport and a validated certificate of health. However, the Slovene authorities required that the document must be issued no more than five days before entering the country. This was a problem as we intended to be on the road for the next five weeks.

Bryn was already thirteen, and Justi had owned him since he was a pup. She'd named him Bryn, which means hill in Welsh, both because he'd been born on a hill farm in mid-Wales and because the house that she lived in at the time shared the same name. They'd soon become inseparable, sharing many days out in the mountains. When Justi met me, the relationship had shifted slightly—I became Bryn's playmate while Justi assumed the role of pack leader and was treated with increased deference—but the three of us were a single, happy unit. We weren't leaving him behind now, even if we had to smuggle him over the border.

Over the summer, we'd managed to put aside the money we'd made at the car boot sales as well as some extra cash from selling possessions that we couldn't take with us, such as the dishwasher. We'd also sold our beloved Canadian canoe that we'd used for many of our adventures, including paddling up remote lochs to reach the more distant hills. With the sale of our Ford Escort too, we'd amassed a grand total of about £1,500 that would have to get us across Europe and last until Justi received her first salary from the school; a possible ten-week timescale. It was going to be tough but not impossible, we thought.

Our day of departure finally arrived, and it was grey and damp, a 'driech' day as they say in the Highlands. We'd had a few friends round for drinks the previous evening for a last chance to say our goodbyes, and neither Justi nor I felt particularly sprightly when we came down for breakfast. As we looked around at the boxes still to be packed and the kitchen cupboards still to be emptied, we remembered with some alarm that 'help' would be arriving shortly. By 'help' what we expected was a well-meaning but somewhat ineffectual distraction in the form of a kind-hearted lady called Hannah.

Hannah, the wife of Justi's manager in the Primary Care Trust, had become a good friend over the last five years, but neither of us had ever considered her to be a very confident or practical person. We'd both fondly witnessed many instances of Hannah's absent-minded, very gentle, very politically correct persona, and we now regretted having accepted her offer of help as the drinks flowed the evening before.

Fortunately, we were about to be shocked and delighted to have our perceived judgement shattered. No sooner had we opened the door to her than Hannah had assessed our bombed-out-warehouse situation and taken militant control. She was a big-framed lady, and we were about to witness the real physical strength that she concealed so well with her gentle and charming behaviour. She ordered us about with authority while taking effective action herself, emptying kitchen cupboards of crockery and cutlery and putting the items into numbered cardboard boxes.

Having finally accomplished all our tasks, we looked at the pile of boxes that Hannah and her husband had agreed to look after for us, now feeling a little guilty about our assumptions of her character.

'Are you sure you don't mind taking these, Hannah, and locking up the house?' asked Justi while I backed up her question with a concerned look and some supportive muttering.

'Yes, it's completely fine,' said Hannah. 'Now get going. You've got a long drive ahead of you.'

The big Renault had managed to swallow our chosen cargo of practical necessities as well as our leisure items. The interior bristled with ice axes, boots, rucksacks and both downhill and cross-country skis, while we had strapped our bikes to the roof rack. Bryn took his place in the passenger footwell, and we wound the windows down to wave goodbye.

My last memory of Birchwood as we pulled out of the driveway was the sight in the car mirror of an efficient Hannah deftly placing heavy book box 'No. 3' into her car boot. We'd never have got away on time if it hadn't been for Hannah.

Late that evening, we arrived in Southport and were greeted by Justi's sister Cath and her husband, Vic, at the rest home that they owned and ran. We'd arranged to base ourselves and all our stuff in their house for the next week or so while we made day trips into Liverpool and Wales to say our goodbyes to family and friends.

Vic helped me unload the bikes from the car and lock them safely in the back yard while Justi and Cath went down to the basement rooms that had been converted into comfortable living accommodation. Bryn was just happy to unfold from the footwell and snuffle about the garden with Cath and Vic's two dogs. Although still game for adventure, he was well past his prime, and we'd both noticed his limbs becoming a little stiff. Maybe a drier climate would be a benefit to all of us, I thought.

As always, and despite the late hour, Cath and Vic had made us a delicious meal, and we chatted excitedly about our plans. They undoubtedly thought we were mad giving up our jobs and home in the Highlands, but they'd always given us encouragement and support in our madcap endeavours. They knew we were drawn to mountainous places, even if they weren't. When we'd told Vic that the average height above sea level in Slovenia was 300m, he'd joked that in Southport it was about one. He and Cath loved the flat fields and marshy coastland with its huge variety of birdlife just as much as we enjoyed the hills.

The next morning, we visited Justi's mum, who by now had determined that it was Slovenia, not Slovakia, we were going to, and she opened her big atlas at a bookmarked page.

'Show me your intended route across Europe,' she suggested.

'Well, it's still a bit sketchy in our minds,' Justi said. 'We plan to take the Dover-Calais ferry and stay with a friend in Brussels before crossing France, Switzerland and Austria and entering Slovenia at one of its north-eastern border crossings.' She pointed out the route to her mother.

'We're hoping to visit Verdun on the way and stop off at scenic places in France such as the Ornans valley and Lauterbrunnen in Switzerland,' I added as Justi traced them in the atlas.

The next ten days whizzed by as we spent time with my folks in Liverpool, visited friends in Wales and completed some last-minute shopping for things we might not find on the way, like loose-leaf tea and marmalade.

On our last evening in the UK, Justi checked her emails on Vic's computer, and a cry of anguish burst from his office.

'What's the matter?'

'The apartment's fallen through! There's a message from one of the school staff saying that the owner has decided to sell it. They say they've found another apartment, but pets aren't allowed.'

We were both deeply upset and unsure of what to do next. While we were grateful for the offer of this second apartment and respected the views of the landlord, Bryn was family to us, and the thought of not having him with us was unthinkable.

A frantic exchange of emails followed as Justi pointed out that we'd jumped through hoops trying to acquire all the documents for Bryn and that it was a bit late in the day for us to find a happy alternative to this housing crisis. The school were obviously trying to negotiate with the new apartment owner, because at 10:30 p.m., they relayed the landlord's last offer. Bryn wouldn't be allowed in the apartment at any time, but he could be housed in the basement garage.

Although it made us both unhappy to imagine Bryn not lying in his basket in our living room, we accepted this last offer as it was equally impossible to contemplate not taking him with us. We also reasoned that we could look for a pet-friendly landlord and change apartments as soon as we found our Slovene feet.

The next day after breakfast, we reloaded the car, which we'd christened the Great White Chariot. Betty arrived to see us off.

'This is it, then,' she said.

She, Cath and Vic waved us off, wondering where and when they'd see us again. Justi had tears in her eyes as we left as it dawned on us for real, maybe for the first time, just how much we were leaving behind.

*****

As we passed just south of Leicester, we left the noise of the busy motorway behind to see if we could get a bite to eat somewhere other than a dreary service station.

'Perfect, there's a pub. Let's see if we can get a snack and a cup of tea,' Justi said as we arrived in a pretty village of granite cottages capped with Swithland slate roofs.

We entered the ancient pub with its low-timbered ceiling, and our eyes took a moment to adjust to the dark interior that smelled of beeswax and ale. Apart from us, there was only one other customer, an elderly man propped on a stool at the end of the bar.

As we ordered tea and sandwiches, the friendly, chatty barmaid asked us where we were heading.

'We're going to Slovenia, to live,' I said.

'Then you'd better take your tin hats with you,' the old man piped up without hesitation. 'They're all killing each other over there.'

It was a recurring theme that we'd heard from quite a few of our friends too—the belief that Slovenia had been, and still was, entangled in the bloody Balkan Wars. In reality, Slovenia was only involved in what had become known as the 'Ten-Day War' when it had stood against the Federal Yugoslav forces, which subsequently withdrew after less than two weeks of limited attacks in 1991, just before the country gained independence.

I tried to explain this to the old boy, but he was adamant that we'd be shot on arrival.

'Don't listen to him,' said the barmaid, rolling her eyes and slipping into her native Leicestershire dialect. 'Ee's a mardy ol' bugger.'

It was dusk when we finally arrived at Dover to discover our ferry was delayed by three hours. Instead of an 8 p.m. crossing, it now meant we wouldn't be arriving at Calais till midnight. Bright floodlights came on and lit the busy port as we walked Bryn along the harbour in search of a café.

Eventually, a green light in the dock informed us it was time to make our way to the border check. I drove while Justi sat in the passenger seat, clutching our passports and a clip file full of Bryn's veterinary documents. The guard wasn't interested in Bryn's papers and waved us through while Justi sighed in relief. Although his documents were legal and above board, we were worried that his health certificate would be invalid well before we reached Slovenia.

We'd arranged to stay with a friend at his apartment in Brussels and, as we didn't own a mobile phone, we couldn't warn him we'd be very late. This troubled us as we knew he had to be up early for work, but as we stood on the deck looking down at the dark water, a strange calm came over us. All the tensions of the last six months seemed to evaporate into the salty night air as the ship's propellers churned the water into a white mass of hissing bubbles and the crew cast the heavy ropes from the moorings. We were overwhelmed with contradictory feelings of both sadness and joy; sad because we were leaving behind all we knew, but joyous because we were embarking on an exciting new adventure.

Chapter 6 Crossing Europe

It had been over ten years since either Justi or I had driven abroad, so we were glad to find the roads relatively quiet as we left Calais behind.

By the time we arrived in Brussels, the city was mostly asleep, but our friend Malachy was waiting up for us. It was 2 a.m., but we chatted for a while, and he graciously made sure we had everything we needed to be comfortable before retiring to bed himself. He had to be at work in less than five hours.

The next day, we had a look around the city and in the evening enjoyed a meal out with Malachy, followed by sampling a few excellent Belgium beers that he proudly recommended.

Malachy is Irish but has lived many years in Brussels, working long hours for the European Commission. He was very interested in our decision to move to Slovenia and believed that the country would most likely become a member of the EU within a few years.

I was pleased to hear this, but because of my situation, I secretly wished a 'few more years' could have been a few more months. Not having a work or residency permit meant, in theory, I would only be allowed into Slovenia for a maximum of three months at any one time. I was expecting to have to go on short camping trips into Austria at the end of every three-month period spent in the country.

'Maybe I should covertly return through a different border checkpoint each time?' I'd said in a dramatic tone to Justi, before adding, 'Don't worry about me, though; I'll take Bryn with me for company.'

'Worry about you? I'd be more worried that Bryn mightn't get back in.'

'Hmmph, and I thought you were my comrade.'

We made our way south, crossing into France and visiting the desperately sad and haunting WW1 battlefields of Verdun, now peaceful and quiet, bathed in warm September sunshine.

We travelled through the amazing limestone rock scenery of the Ornans river valley and through many beautiful French towns and villages, happy to avoid driving on monotonous motorways. Each night, we pitched our tent at one of the municipal campsites that every town seemed to have. They were clean, well-kept and cheap too. Being late summer, we mostly had them to ourselves.

We'd buy a lunchtime snack at local markets or grocery stores, and each evening I'd cook a one-pan meal on our camping Gaz stove. I'd honed my one-pan cooking skills through years of camping and staying in Highland bothies. We had tasty risottos and pastas, spicy curried rice and savoury stews; all of them costing no more than a few euros each day.

We crossed the border into Switzerland near Basel, driving through spectacular landscapes and over steep little passes before arriving at the stunningly scenic Lauterbrunnen valley. The giants of the Bernese Oberland—the Eiger, Mönch and Jungfrau—lay close by to the east.

Justi and I had visited this beautiful valley together on a cycle camping trip four years earlier, and we were eager to break our journey there for a few days and enjoy some walking.

We found a campsite below the steep rock walls of the valley, where shimmering waterfalls cascaded from their tops. It was one of my all-time favourite places, and I wondered if Slovenia had a valley to match its beauty.

In the 1980s, I'd climbed a peak called the Tschingelhorn, and I remembered that the approach path to the mountain passed a small but beautiful lake high above the end of the valley. I suggested to Justi that we should go and find it the next day.

We made an early start and began the long walk up the narrow road that leads to the headwall of the Lauterbrunnen valley. Sensible folk take the post bus, but having spent so much time driving, we were keen to stretch our legs and get some much-needed exercise.

Bryn was happy to get moving again too, and he was enjoying all the smells and sensations of an alpine valley, where cows and goats grazed happily in the meadows. He lingered longer than usual at every cowpat, admiring the bouquet like a canine connoisseur who'd chanced upon an interesting vintage.

It was a longer walk than I remembered, and after two hours, we'd only just reached the head of the valley. We both felt unfit; we hadn't had much spare time for hillwalking in the six months before leaving the Highlands. However, I'd promised Justi that it would be well worth the effort to see the beautiful turquoise lake of my memories.

And so we began the 900-metre ascent to reach the Obersteinberg hotel. By 2 p.m., the steep path finally levelled out, and we reached the hotel—a large old wooden chalet. One of the upstairs shutters snapped open, and a man wearing a feathered cap stuck his head out. I half expected him to say, 'Cuckoo!'

By now, Justi seemed to have lost interest in my 'lovely lake', and I hoped she wouldn't see the sign before I'd arranged some refreshments, but it was too late.

'An hour, another hour to the lake. Just a stroll, to stretch our legs you said.'

'Look, we've done all the hard work now. It's relatively easy from here. Let's get a cup of tea and a strudel.'

Sitting on a bench outside the hotel, we took in the incredible Alpine vista of the Bernese Oberland while Bryn lapped water from a large bowl provided by the hotel and lay down contentedly in the shade at our feet.

Snow-capped giants, including the Jungfrau, Wetterhorn and Briethorn, glistened and shimmered in the afternoon sunshine, and the sound of cowbells drifted in the sweet, clear air.

'All right,' said Justi. 'Let's do it then. Maybe I could cool my feet in your wonderful turquoise tarn.'

As we neared the lake, I strode on ahead, anticipating the stunning scene of its cold, crystal-clear water cupped in its mountain setting. I ascended the low moraine that held back the lake and peered over the edge into what looked like a green, muddy puddle.

Justi soon joined me, and she wasn't impressed. Even Bryn, who showed enthusiasm for most things involving walks, didn't look impressed. It had been a particularly dry summer, and the normally sparkling lake had shrivelled to a fraction of its capacity.

We sat on a boulder as Bryn muddied his paws in the green slime. It was still a fantastic location, though, and we hoped that the little lake would soon regain its looks in the autumn rains.

It was almost dark as we arrived back at the campsite, feeling weary but elated too. We vowed not to neglect our fitness for such a long period again.

We stayed in the valley for a few days more and enjoyed a second fabulous walk. Although it was another lengthy hike, this time we made it easier by using public transport to gain height first. We took the train up to Kleine Scheidegg, a famous pass that lies below the north face of the Eiger, Mönch and Jungfrau, then walked back down to Lauterbrunnen past the mountain village of Wengen, perched on its grassy alp. It was another beautiful sunny day, and we wished we had the time and money to extend our stay.

We continued north through Switzerland on minor roads, being careful to avoid the expensive motorway tolls but also just wanting to enjoy the scenery. The overloaded Great White Chariot struggled gallantly over a steep pass into the little principality of Lichtenstein before dropping down into Austria, where we followed a broad open valley heading towards Innsbruck.

Justi wanted to visit Achensee, a lake (much larger than mine!) in the Austrian Tyrol to the north-east of Innsbruck, which had inspired the early writings of Elinor M. Brent-Dyer. She was the author of a series of children's books about the Chalet School which Justi had read as a child. There are 58 books in the Chalet School series, and the stories about the girls' adventures in the Alps had helped ignite Justi's interest in mountains.

Elinor had holidayed at Achensee in the 1920s, and although she never revisited the Alps, her memories of the Tyrol inspired her writing until she died in 1969. We found a campsite near the lake and spent the next day walking along the lakeshore and visiting some of the locations that Justi recognised from the books. At times, when the old steam train chugged past and tourists waved to us from one of the small cruise boats, it appeared not much had changed in the 80 years or so since the first book had been penned.

*****

It was now almost the end of September, and it was apparent that the summer holiday season was nearing its end. For every campsite still open, several had already closed for the winter. It had been an enjoyable trip, but the minor niggles and discomforts of camping were beginning to tell, and we longed to have a bed in a place of our own again as we were effectively homeless.

The weather was also beginning to change, with rain forecast for the following week, so we decided to push on and make one more stop in Austria before driving over the border into Slovenia.

We were anxious about Bryn's health certificate no longer being valid for the Slovene authorities, and although neither of us said anything, we both imagined a nightmare scenario where we were refused entry at the border. So far, we hadn't had to produce any of Bryn's documents at any time during the journey. That didn't stop us from feeling worried, though, and as we approached each border crossing, a tense, silent atmosphere pervaded the Great White Chariot.

On our last night in Austria, we managed to find a small campsite not far from the town of Völkermarkt. After we'd pitched the tent and had some dinner, we heard the unmistakable sound of an oompah band strike up, so we wandered along the road to investigate. The band was playing outdoors on a large well-constructed stage and had drawn a sizeable crowd. There was something familiar about the traditional costume they were all dressed in, but I wasn't sure what, or why I'd even noticed.

'They're Slovenes!' Justi exclaimed. 'Look at that poster; it's a Slovene band.'

We'd both seen images of traditional Slovene costumes during our fact-finding missions, and the band's outfits jogged our memories. They wore the brightly coloured silk shawls that protrude like fringed epaulettes from under their waistcoats, dark breeches, polished black leather boots and on their heads, black felt caps decorated with a red carnation.

The music was excellent. To dismissively call it 'oompah' is a terrible injustice and an indicator of my ignorance when it comes to ethnic alpine music styles. During the interlude, we chatted to one of the musicians who confirmed that they were, indeed, Slovene. He seemed surprised but very proud when we told him we were moving to his country.

'The Julian Alps are the finest mountains,' he said. 'I live in Gorenjska, near Triglav. You should go there.'

The Austrian crowd loved every minute of the concert and gave thundering applause to each solo clarinet or accordion melody. One of the tunes (called 'Na Golici') sounded very familiar, and so it should. It was written by Slovenia's best-known folk musician, Slavko Avsenik, and is known in English as 'Trumpet Echoes'. It's considered to be the most played instrumental song in the world.

*****

The next day, we packed the tent away as rain started to fall from a grey, leaden sky. It felt as if summer had just declared itself over for another year.

Justi and I had developed into a slick team over the last month of driving. As well as navigating, the passenger would cover for the blind spots that the right-hand drive configuration of our UK car caused. We found ourselves needing that teamwork as the rain became heavier, the roads busier and the visibility decreased. With the windscreen wipers going into overdrive and the de-misters on full, the Great White Chariot splashed along Austria's southern boundary.

The names of Slovene towns had been appearing on road signs for a while now, and we knew we must be getting close to the border, but it was difficult to judge the distances on the well-used road atlas Justi had on her lap.

Suddenly, as we exited a roundabout, an overhead road sign looming out of the wet, grey sky read 'Republic of Slovenia 500m'. This was it! Justi hurriedly gathered our passports and Bryn's documents together, but we were waved through the Austrian control and into no man's land without needing to stop.

Feeling sick with nerves, Justi wound down her window as we slowed to a stop at the Slovene border station.

Chapter 7 First Impressions

Two Slovene border guards sat in the control kiosk, and one of them stood up slowly and drew the partition window open a little wider.

Bryn was lying under Justi's outstretched legs in the footwell and, being almost entirely black, he was practically invisible against the dark carpet of the car. The tension was palpable as both of us willed Bryn not to move and catch the guard's attention.

Justi stretched out her arm and handed the guard our passports while she balanced Bryn's file of documents ready on her knee. The guard gave the passports a cursory glance before handing them back promptly to her. Then, with a friendly smile, we were waved through yet another border. We'll never know if the guard had noticed Bryn or wondered about the file of documents on Justi's knee, but at that moment, we didn't care anymore. All the stress and tension over Bryn's technically invalid certificate dissipated, and we both felt like a great weight had been lifted from us. We were finally in Slovenia!

Bryn stirred, scratched his ear and then dozed on peacefully, blissfully unaware of borders, rules and customs regulations.

It was early afternoon on a Sunday, and we were about an hour's drive from the spa town. The school weren't expecting us until Monday, and we didn't have any way of letting them know of our early arrival. However, Justi had printed out all the emails she'd received from the school before we left the UK, and one of them showed the name and address of the teacher who was to be her mentor. We decided to drive to the town and try to find her.

The rain had eased a little, but low clouds hung over the land like a thick grey blanket. The Slovene road signs and billboards bore names and words that appeared very alien to us; the language didn't have any of the similarities that we'd got used to in the countries we'd been driving through for the last month.

We continued through undulating rural countryside trying to get our first glimpses of the new country that we hoped would become our home. Between breaks in the dense beech forests, we saw small fields, some supporting several cattle. In one or two fields, the cows were attached to a long piece of chain that was tethered to a wooden stake driven into the ground. They could each graze a circle of about ten metres in the lush, wet grass.

The biggest fields contained a farmstead, and close to the house stood large open-frame structures that looked like a type of barn. They were constructed of ancient timbers, huge beams of dry, gnarled wood, and some of them leaned at alarming angles. We could see hay stored in the upper part, and the outer frames were hung with cobs of corn, the bright yellow kernels adding a dash of colour to the misty grey weather. We later discovered that these open barns, called *toplar*, are unique to, and typical of, eastern Slovenia.

The towns and villages we passed through seemed very quiet; as it was Sunday, all the shops were closed. The only signs of activity we noticed were from people seated in the warmly lit bars and restaurants called *gostilna*. We suspected that the Slovenes enjoyed getting together for their Sunday dinner.

The houses were mostly large two- or three-storey detached buildings, and almost all had a neat vegetable garden. Each town also had a few modern-looking apartment blocks five or six storeys high, and even these had what looked like neat vegetable allotments adjacent to the residents' parking areas. Most properties had roller blinds on the windows—a testament to bright sunny weather, we hoped.

As we approached the spa town, Podpetek, we passed a big sign that read '*Dobrodošli*—Welcome!'

We began to look out for the name of the area where Justi's mentor lived and, by chance, spotted it almost immediately. We swung left off the road and found ourselves in a residential street with a small apartment block at its end. I parked the car and switched the engine off. A young man walked past staring quizzically at our car, first at its number plate and then at Justi, before shifting his gaze to me sitting behind a wheel that wasn't on the usual side. He smirked, probably thinking we were a couple of lost tourists.

'I think she must live in one of those apartments,' said Justi.

We locked the car and made our way to the small block of flats, where we checked the names and numbers on the list in the entrance passage.

'This is it, right here on the ground floor,' said Justi, moving towards a brightly coloured apartment door. A lady answered the door and stood silently for a moment, her mind quickly trying to translate and process the information as Justi introduced us both.

'You are Yoosti? But you will arrive tomorrow.'

'Yes. I'm sorry. We are a day early, but we couldn't phone to let you know as we haven't got your number,' Justi explained, adding with a smile, 'I'm Justi, by the way, not Yoosti.'

'Ah, we pronounce 'J' as a 'Y' here in Slovenia. Come in, come in, I will have to make some phone calls.'

She ushered us into her hallway and offered us both a pair of slippers from a basket full of different sizes. At first, I declined but quickly changed my mind after a sharp nudge in the ribs from Justi suggested I'd got it wrong.

'I think it must be the done thing,' Justi whispered as we were led into the living room to sit at a table. The table was surrounded by cardboard boxes and heaps of clip files; the boxes and files bulged with written papers and exercise books.

The lady introduced herself as Jelka and apologised for the clutter, saying that she didn't have enough space in her small apartment for all the school work she regularly brought home. She made us some tea and coffee, and we chatted for a while as we explained our decision to arrive a day early. She understood our not wanting to spend another night in a wet tent and picked up her phone, saying she'd contact our new landlords to let them know we'd arrived. After a brief conversation, she hung up and told us that the apartment wouldn't be ready until noon the next day. She recommended a hotel on the main street that offered reasonable out-of-season prices. We thanked her for the tip as we were both eager to spend a comfortable first night in Slovenia after weeks of camping on our thin, roll-up mattresses.

Jelka said that she would round up the troops (we've often found since then that Slovenes love to use English idioms, not always as correctly as Jelka) and ask another of the English teachers to meet us for a meal in town later that evening. We left Jelka amid her piles of school work after she'd contacted her colleague and arranged that they would meet us at the hotel at 7 p.m.

We drove past the town centre and soon found ourselves back on a quiet rural road. We stopped at a gravel parking area on the edge of a forest to give Bryn a walk.

A broad track led through beautiful tall beech woods, their silvery grey bark glistening in the rain. Narrower paths crossed our track and headed off deep into the enchanting wood. There didn't appear to be any access restrictions, and the only signs we'd seen at the parking area depicted people in athletic positions exercising on a variety of outdoor gym equipment.

Bryn disappeared down one of the narrow side paths, but we weren't concerned that he'd get lost. Whenever he walked off lead, he would run ahead for about 50 metres then return to round us up and keep his herd moving along in typical collie fashion. Anxious to keep him close for his first walk on Slovene soil, we called him, and after a few seconds, he came bounding back. He wasn't happy about moving on quite yet, though, and he stood looking back along the track.

'Come on then, what have you found?' I asked as it was apparent he'd seen something of interest. A few metres down the track, he stopped at the base of a tree to show us the object of his attention.

'Wow, just look at that; it's amazing,' Justi exclaimed as a slow-moving amphibious creature climbed between the twigs and leaves on the muddy track. It was our first sighting of a fire salamander with its shiny black body covered in bright yellow blotches. Bryn was instinctively sensible not to touch it as some salamanders can secrete powerful toxins from their skin.

Happy that he'd successfully introduced us to his slippery friend, Bryn led us back to the main track in an eager search for more new things.

We returned to town and pulled into one of the long parking strips that ran parallel to the high street. We knew we must be close to the rear of the hotel that Jelka had recommended. Bryn jumped up onto the passenger seat, as he always did when we left him in the car, and curled up happily, tucking his nose into his tail in preparation for another doze.

The style of the hotel surprised us both. We entered the foyer through an impressive revolving door, all glass and brass and smelling of polish. A smiling receptionist stood behind an imposing, marble-topped desk.

'Hello, do you speak English?' I asked.

'Yes, of course. Would you like a room?' she asked in flawless English.

Podpetek spa town was a place that received a high proportion of international guests, and I imagined English would often be the common denominator, the language used by many.

'Yes, please. Er, can we bring our dog in?'

'No, I'm sorry. That is not possible. Do you still want the room?'

Justi and I looked at each other and agreed that he'd be fine in the car overnight. Bryn had become quite used to sleeping in the car on the trip over as our tent was a small two-person dome with barely enough space for ourselves. He probably got the better deal on rainy nights.

After accepting the room, a porter wearing a starched white jacket and dark trousers appeared seemingly from nowhere and picked up our case. 'Please,' he said, indicating the way and leading us up a wide staircase to our second-floor room. We followed behind, grinning at the stark contrast of our little tent to the colonial-style decoration and opulence of the old hotel. The room was in the same style—cream-coloured walls and elegant, dark wood furniture with regal-looking pillars either side of an arched window frame.

We looked out onto the main pedestrian thoroughfare as the street lamps came on, dispersing their light through a colourful corona in the foggy twilight. Suddenly, a door opened in one of the buildings opposite, and a large man in a white dressing gown came out with a towel over his arm. He sniffed the damp evening air then sauntered nonchalantly up the middle of the road before disappearing into another doorway. A moment later, two ladies, also wearing dressing gowns and carrying towels, walked up the road chatting before disappearing into the same doorway.

'What do you reckon *that's* all about?' I asked Justi.

'I think it might be something to do with the spas.'

'I hope you're right,' I said, intrigued but feeling slightly uneasy. 'It would be a bit odd if it wasn't.'

After checking on Bryn, we waited in the foyer for Jelka, who arrived with her colleague Nina and Nina's husband, Dejan (pronounced Dayan). They invited us to a pizza restaurant a little way up the main road. As we walked up the road chatting, we noticed the doorway the white-robed figures had made for—it was a swimming pool and was, indeed, part of the spa complex. Other buildings advertised their services within as gyms, massage parlours and a whole plethora of health-treatment boutiques.

We filed into the warm and inviting pizza restaurant where we were greeted by Sara, the owner, who led us to our table. As we ordered beers, Sara asked about our coming to Slovenia, listening with interest as we told her about our hopes to visit the Julian Alps. Sara's husband, Alaz, joined us, and they shared their own story about how they'd come to be in Podpetek.

It was a far more dramatic and harrowing tale than our leisurely drive across the continent. Sara was Slovene but had lived in Sweden during the 1980s, where she'd met Alaz, an Iraqi Kurd, who had fled his country as a teenager during the years when Saddam Hussein was committing genocide against the Kurdish people. Having lost members of his family and in fear for his own life, Alaz was forced to make a perilous journey north, travelling on a mule across deserts and over mountains. He didn't even have a passport but somehow managed to finally make his way to Sweden where he was given asylum as a refugee. After Sara and Alaz met and married, she suggested they should move to Slovenia to make a new life. They'd since gained a fantastic reputation with both tourists and Slovenes alike for the wonderful food, friendliness and atmosphere of their little restaurant. It was even mentioned in our *Lonely Planet* guide.

As we chatted, waiting for our order, we drank our first Slovene beers. There are two main beers found throughout Slovenia—Laško with a green label and Union with a red one. Our new friends insisted that the former was the best. Laško, the town where the beer is brewed, also happened to be not far from Podpetek, so we joked about possible bias and vowed we'd try the Union too, just to be fair. We clinked our glasses to the Slovene salutation of '*Nazdravje!*'

We talked about the apartment that we would be moving into, and both Jelka and Nina assured us it was beautiful and spacious, though maybe rather overpriced. The owners were renting it out for the first time and had proven to be a little demanding in their dealings with the school admin staff.

I discovered that Dejan, a manager in the local glass factory, was a keen road cyclist. When I shared my passion for riding and told him I'd brought my bike, he invited me to join him and his friends for group rides at weekends.

And so the evening continued with warm conservation and the most delicious pizzas and pasta we'd ever had. Our new friends wouldn't let us offer anything towards the bill; they seemed almost offended that we'd offered.

'We invited you, so we will pay. That is how it is in Slovenia,' they told us.

Despite the grey and wet weather, Justi and I felt uplifted and excited to see what the next day would bring in our new country.

Chapter 8 Struggles

The following morning, we looked out of the window into a thick blanket of grey. The fog seemed to have got worse, but at least it was no longer raining. After seeing to Bryn, we enjoyed a breakfast of *pršut* (air-dried ham) with freshly baked rolls and croissants at a table instead of having it on our knees in the car or crouching in the tent. That's not to say that we hadn't enjoyed our alfresco dining experiences, but it felt good to indulge in a little luxury.

Collecting Bryn again from the car, we went to have a look around the town. The beautiful old square and park were surrounded by grand neoclassical buildings which were mostly used as hotels and private apartments. We saw the lovely corner building, now for sale, where the first apartment offered to us had been, and hoped that the second one would be as nice.

On the way, we'd seen a few more folk in their dressing gowns and sandals. They strolled past purposefully, en route to their next appointment in the quest to cure all their ills and to feel good—and why not, we thought.

It all seemed quite surreal to us, though, as they appeared out of the fog, clutching their towels, chatting or maybe whistling a tune, while local people in suits, overalls and uniforms went about their daily business. It felt as though we'd accidentally stumbled onto the set of one those 1960s TV fantasy dramas like *The Prisoner* or *The Avengers*. However, it was obviously just another day in the life of a spa town, and over the months we would get used to it.

The buildings of the square backed onto the wooded slope of a small hill. We found a gravel parking area with information boards that showed walking routes up the hill and, again, picture signs of people using exercise equipment.

'We've got a couple of hours of free time. Let's take a walk up our first Slovene hill,' Justi suggested.

Neither Bryn nor I needed any persuading; it felt good to get moving again. It was still foggy, but we started climbing a wide, well-trodden path through the wood and almost immediately met people in tracksuits coming down and one or two passing us on the way up. They were all using Nordic walking poles and moving at a steady, rhythmic pace. In a small clearing, we came across more folk using some of the exercise equipment we'd seen on the car park information board. We heard some of them before we saw them, their grunts and groans giving them away as they used the vaulting bars, rings on ropes, and rubber tyres spaced out on the ground, all with detailed signs showing how they should be used.

As we reached the top, the path levelled and appeared to continue along the narrow spine of the wooded hill, but we decided to save that walk for another day. An observation tower stood on the summit as the trees obscured any view. We looped Bryn's lead around one of its legs and began ascending the steep metal staircase. On and up we went, the tower moving and swaying alarmingly with every step until we were well above the tallest trees.

We weren't expecting to see anything on such a foggy day, but as we stepped onto the viewing platform, we found ourselves in clear, bright air. We looked out onto a sea of cloud with forested hills poking through like dark islands as far as the eye could see. Some of the hilltops had been cleared of forest, and many of them were adorned with small churches or chapels. We looked out in the direction of Croatia as the border was very close. It was exciting to imagine nipping into Croatia for the day, although the landscape looked very similar from this viewpoint.

We carefully made our way back down to the bottom of the steps, glad to see Bryn again as he'd been completely out of sight in the mist. We later discovered that many forested summits in eastern Slovenia have a metal viewing tower, some of them surprisingly high. They often feel unnervingly rickety, but I'm sure that the movement is an engineering safety feature in the event of strong winds.

We discovered more equipment along the track as it made a loop back down through the woods to the car park. We'd read that the Slovene people valued health and leisure equally, and we wondered if the locals used these facilities as much as the tourists and visitors to the spa.

We'd arranged to meet our new landlady at midday at the school, where we would sign a three-month rental contract as the school had agreed to contribute to our payments. In such a small town, we had no difficulty in locating the school, which was a primary for kids six to fourteen years old. It had a capacity of about 700 pupils, with children commuting in from many of the tiny hill villages and small valley populations of the area.

We were met at the door by Jelka who led us along a corridor to an office. Our new landlady was already there and stood up to shake hands as we entered. She introduced herself by simply stating her name, Rozalija, and we did the same, having learned the previous evening that it's the Slovene way. There are little of the British niceties or small talk when you meet Slovenes for the first time, but it makes it easier to remember people's names.

Rozalija was tall and elegant, dressed in an expensive-looking jacket and skirt with stiletto ankle boots. She was a fashion designer who divided her hours between working at home and commuting into her office in Ljubljana.

We are neither tall nor elegant, and having just returned from our walk, we were wearing fleece jackets, trekking pants and muddy training shoes. I could sense that we hadn't yet scored a point on Rozalija's approval-ratings index.

Jelka translated the details of the three-month rental contract, but before anyone signed it, Rozalija wanted to add a verbal agreement. She insisted that we must make an extra payment for any guests we might invite to stay overnight. We didn't feel this last-minute clause was a particularly fair one. From what the others had said, we were already paying over the odds for the apartment. Just before we'd left the UK, Cath and Vic had suggested that, once we were settled, they would come out for a visit and bring Betty too. We'd planned to accommodate Betty while Cath and Vic booked into a spa hotel. We had no choice but to accept Rozalija's unreasonable demand and sign the contract, but we both silently vowed that we would start looking for another apartment at the first opportunity.

Having completed the formalities, we followed behind Rozalija's black sports car to be shown our new residence. Her home was located near the end of a residential street that looked similar to many we'd seen in other towns the day before. It was a large two-storey house with a garage and basement built partly into the ground. We parked our travel-dirty, overladen White Chariot next to Rozalija's shiny set of wheels.

A low-maintenance, landscaped garden surrounded the house without any sign of the vegetable plots we could see in neighbouring gardens. In one section of the garden, there was a big metal cage with a kennel inside. A huge dog, similar to a Newfoundland, emerged from the kennel and put his nose between the cage bars to get a closer look at the new arrivals. Rozalija's husband, Marko, came out to greet us; he was an athletic-looking man, sporting the unshaven Beckham look, his shirt open enough to see the large gold medallion on his chest. He shook our hands and introduced himself, but like Rozalija, he seemed a little cold and looked at us disapprovingly.

Opening the garage doors, he said, 'Your dog can stay here,' pointing to a corner of the concrete floor. A large BMW saloon car filled most of the garage, and I wondered how I'd squeeze Bryn's bed in beside it.

I opened the car and got Bryn's basket out of the rear and then let him out to meet his new hosts. Rosalija wasn't interested in meeting a muddy-pawed old collie. Marko was keen to show that he was the pack leader in this household and ordered Bryn to come to him. But Bryn had by now wandered towards the cage to make friends with the donkey-sized fur ball within.

'Ha, your dog needs to be trained,' said Marko.

I could see Justi's hackles rise in response to his comment.

'Bryn is very well trained, thank you,' she snapped, sounding both angry and hurt at once. Justi had begun training Bryn from the moment she got him, and he had been eager to learn. As well as all the usual commands most dogs can follow, she'd taught him never to jump a wall or swim in water until she told him he could. As a young dog, she'd taken him on long hill walks in sheep country, so it was important that he never jumped over a wall or fence first in case there was livestock on the other side. He'd been trained to sit and wait whenever he came to a stile too, until Justi gave him the command to cross it.

Swimming was his favourite thing, but Justi had taught him, for safety, never to enter water until she allowed it. He would stand, quivering with excitement on a riverbank or sandy beach, looking pleadingly towards the water and waiting for the call of assent, 'In you go.'

We'd noticed, though, that in the last year or so, Bryn sometimes seemed not to hear a low-voiced command, and we wondered if he was losing his hearing.

Marko went over to the cage and let his dog out. We were a bit apprehensive for a moment, but Bryn and Marko's huge dog, Simba, immediately became friends. They sniffed happily around the garden together until Marko ordered Simba back into his cage. Marko had excellent control over his dog, but it seemed a bit harsh to us that he was permanently confined outdoors.

With Bryn now shut in the garage, we were shown inside to our apartment. Having learned Slovene slipper decorum at Jelka's, we took our shoes off in the hall and made our selection from the wicker box that contained about ten pairs of slippers especially for guests.

Rozalija and Marko lived on the ground floor, and we were to have the upstairs rooms. We followed Rozalija upstairs, passing carefully arranged vases of imitation irises and modern art paintings, the polished tile floor gleaming. The apartment was lovely—a modern kitchen-dining room, two good-sized bedrooms with fitted wardrobes, and a very spacious living room. This last was furnished with a six-seat corner sofa and a TV cabinet. The TV was a tiny portable one, and it looked very odd in such a huge room. It sat on its cabinet on one side of the room, looking detached and distant from the sofa on the other side.

We would have to supply bedding and all kitchen utensils. We hadn't been expecting that and wondered how much it would diminish what we had left of our savings. A washing machine was to be supplied and fitted by the school the next day. It was arranged that I would meet the school janitor and help him bring the machine up to the apartment. Washing machines are almost always fitted in bathrooms in Slovenia, which makes a lot more sense than placing them in the kitchen, where most are found in the UK.

Rozalija handed us the apartment keys, and we headed into town to buy what we needed. In 2002, there were only two major supermarket retailers in Slovenia. One of them had an offshoot store that sold electrical goods, furniture and household items and, luckily for us, Podpetek was a big enough town to have one.

At the time, Slovenia didn't have the euro, and the currency was the tolar. One pound sterling equated to about 310 tolars, and, initially, we found it difficult and confusing to make the conversion in our minds for every item we bought. The checkout bill was depressing, despite carefully choosing the best-value deals, and we knew we would be struggling to make ends meet before Justi received her first salary.

Once back at the house, we began to carry our newly acquired goods upstairs, but no sooner had we entered the hallway than Rozailja popped out of her doorway. We peered over the duvets and pillows we were loaded with to see Rozalija, looking stern with hands on hips, telling us to put slippers on.

'Yes, of course, sorry,' I said as we both struggled blindly to kick our shoes off and step into the slippers without having to put everything on the floor. We followed a carefully choreographed sequence of swapping shoes and slippers each time we left and entered the house, and we could sense Rozalija was somehow watching our every move.

Having stocked the apartment, we went down to the garage to see how Bryn was managing and to take him for a walk. He was waiting behind the garage door, eager to be with his pack mates again. We felt frustrated and hopeless that he couldn't be with us in the apartment.

As we walked him down the street, a cacophony of barking erupted as we passed several houses that also had caged dogs in the garden. Most of them were German shepherds or Dobermans, all looking and sounding very aggressive as they barked at Bryn, the new kid on the block. Luckily, it wasn't long before we found ourselves on a quiet rural track where we could all breathe a sigh of relief. Although the guard dogs were well secured in their cages, we'd found their aggression distressing, and Bryn had pulled hard on his lead in fear to get away from the street as fast as possible.

That evening, as we sat in the big empty-feeling space of the apartment, Justi started to cry uncontrollably.

'What on earth have we done? I'd rather we lived in a bus shelter as long as we were all together,' she sobbed.

We both felt mentally tired out from the trials of our first day, and we wondered how we would cope if this was how our time in Slovenia was to continue.

Chapter 9 Dazed and Confused

After the tiresome struggles of the previous day, Justi and I finally collapsed into the wonderfully comfortable bed, the best thing in our new apartment, and fell into a deep slumber. Stressful situations can often seem better after a good night's sleep, and we both awoke feeling refreshed and ready to face the new day.

Justi was due to start her job at the school at 7:30 a.m., so we jumped up to put the kettle on and make breakfast. Apart from a loaf of bread and some milk and butter in the fridge, the cupboards were bare, so one of my jobs that morning was to do some shopping. First, I'd give Bryn a good walk, and I was anxious to test something out on the local guard dog community.

As I was unpacking some of our luggage late the previous evening, I'd noticed the small box that contained our dog Dazer. The Dazer was a small, hand-held device that we'd bought after having been chased and nipped on the ankles by a wild-eyed little terrier on one our cycling tours. The device emitted a harmless, high-frequency sound that only dogs can hear and caused a dog in pursuit to falter for a second or two while you pedalled away faster than Lance Armstrong being chased by the UCI doping squad, or so the blurb on the box read. Since buying it, we hadn't found the need to use it, but that was about to change.

With Justi off to work, I let Bryn out of his solitary confinement, and we headed out to face the barks and howls of the street's canine choristers. I held the Dazer inconspicuously in my free hand as I held on tight to Bryn's lead with the other.

A deep, almighty WOOF! from a big Alsatian made me jump and caused Bryn to start pulling strongly on the lead, something he never did in normal circumstances. I aimed the Dazer in the direction of the baritone Alsatian and squeezed the button. The big dog immediately stopped woofing and stood looking at us with a befuddled expression.

It was a similar scenario with the next two barking brutes; one even started wagging its tail as though it had forgotten its profession for a moment. The road soon became quiet except for the odd Scooby Doo-style whimper.

There was just one more dog to pass at the end of the street; one that had startled Justi and me the day before, not because it was large or aggressive, but because of its behaviour. It was actually quite a small dog which contributed to the canine clamour by impressively jumping ten times its height to see over the fence. Its head would appear for a few seconds above the top of the tall garden fence at regular intervals before disappearing again. It was as though it was on a trampoline, and each time it was briefly suspended at its apex height, it would yap once.

I couldn't resist. As we passed the house, I managed to blip the Dazer at the optimum time. The dog stopped in mid-yelp and seemed to be suspended in flight for a little longer than usual. With an extremely perplexed look on its furry face, it descended out of sight and failed to reappear. I never saw the little dog again, ever. Don't be alarmed, gentle reader; although he seemed to have given up his trampoline routine, I regularly heard him yapping in excitement as his owner played with him in his garden.

Even to this day, I've never really understood the Slovenes' need to keep a caged guard dog to protect their properties as the crime rate in the country is extremely low compared to, say, the UK's. They bark at anything and everyone at the drop of a hat, and any potential burglar can see they're caged.

After a good long hike with Bryn through fields and forest, I returned to the apartment to have a cup of tea and write a shopping list. I opened the fridge door and was surprised to find its sparse contents had been augmented by something I didn't recognise and which was oddly disturbing.

What looked like a strange mound of haggis lay on a plate on one of the shelves. Rough wooden skewers pierced and tied the ends of the skin sack of the sheep's stomach enclosing it. I couldn't understand how this strange-looking item had mysteriously arrived in our fridge. I struggled to make any rational sense of it and imagined it could be something sinister; a warning perhaps, an ancient rural Slovene ritual to scare incomers who try and silence their hell hounds.

Who else had a key to our apartment apart from our landlords, who had both left for work before we had? After checking the apartment for goats' heads and effigies, I pondered over the puzzle while I drank my tea and came to the conclusion that, indeed, it must be a warning from the Podpetek satanic society.

Putting my irrational concerns aside, I went to the local shops to buy the week's groceries. Supermarkets are pretty much the same in most European countries, but the layout and choice of items can vary a lot. There was an abundance of fresh salad and seasonal vegetables and shelves of pickled preserves. There were large pots of sauerkraut, tubs of *skuta* (Slovene cottage cheese), a wonderful selection of home-baked breads and handmade biscuits, scrumptious-looking cakes and a deli counter full of air-dried meats. I made a mental note to try and remember the locations of all the everyday items like milk, bread and vegetables. I struggled with the Slovene food names, but after about 30 minutes, I'd managed to fill my shopping bag with food to last till the weekend.

Just before midday, I made my way to meet the janitor who was to help us deliver and fit the washing machine that had been supplied by the school. As I walked into the school reception area, a few kids walked past, giggling and pointing at me saying, 'Hello, Meester English.' News travels fast in small towns, and it sometimes feels as though you're wearing a large neon flashing sign declaring, 'Yes, I'm foreign.' If all goes well, the sign eventually begins to lose its novelty factor, and you become at least accepted, if not exactly a local.

Primož, the janitor, came to meet me and motioned me to follow him to his workshop where he already had the washing machine on a portable trolley. He handed me a bag full of flexible hoses and pipe joints saying, 'Vee go to combi,' as he leaned the trolley back and balanced the weight of the machine on its wheels. He had a kindly face and a humorous glint in his eye and, although it had started raining again, he seemed pleased to be getting out of the school for a while to do something a bit different from his normal job routine. Between us, we heaved the heavy washer into the back of his combi van and headed off to the house. Thankfully, he already knew the way, as I suspect he wouldn't have understood directions from me in English.

Rozaljia's car was parked outside, and I remembered that she'd said something the day before about returning from work to oversee the washing machine installation. It was raining heavily as we unloaded the machine and struggled up the short flight of steps to the front door. No sooner had we manoeuvred the machine into the hallway than Rozalija appeared from her doorway.

'No shoes. Put sleeepers on!' she ordered. With his back to Rozalija, Primož rolled his eyes, swapping a look with me that transcended any need for translation. We lowered the machine carefully to the floor, kicked off our shoes and made our selection from the slipper box. Rozalija went ahead, attempting to direct us around the sharp turns on the stairs and generally getting in the way. Once we'd successfully positioned the washing machine in the bathroom, Rozalija left us in peace and went back to work while Primož began connecting the pipes to the machine. I invited him to come through to the kitchen and have some coffee and biscuits I'd organised. Sitting down at the table, Primož took a sip and pulled a face.

'You don't like the coffee?' I said, gesturing towards the jar of instant that we'd brought with us from the UK.

'Dat ees not coffee.'

Having already enjoyed a few excellent cups of freshly made Slovene coffee in the pizza restaurant and the hotel, I believe he had a point.

Justi arrived home at 2 p.m., having completed a successful first day at the school. It was nice to know we still had the rest of the afternoon to explore the area and that some days she would finish work as early as noon.

As she told me about her day, I wondered how I'd break the news about the mysterious pagan intruder stealing into the apartment and leaving something sinister in the fridge.

'Did you find the black-pudding thingy?' Justi asked enthusiastically.

'Black pudding?'

'Yes, it was one of many presents the kids gave me,' she said, pointing to a carrier bag full of chocolates and biscuits that she'd brought home. 'It's a gift from one of the children's grandmothers. I brought it back and popped it in the fridge during my morning break to keep it fresh.'

Justi went on to explain how she'd been told that, at this time of year, many Slovenes who own a pig slaughter and butcher it. They call the practice *koline*, and every part of the animal that's not immediately eaten is preserved by salting, smoking or drying.

'It's a great honour to share your *koline* with a stranger, apparently, and even though we don't eat much meat, it's a very hospitable gesture.'

'Ah, I see,' I said, feeling both ridiculous and grateful at the same time. 'At least we won't have to draw a pentagram around the bed tonight.'

'What?'

'Oh, nothing...'

*****

By the end of our first week in Slovenia, we'd begun the process of piecing together all the strange new experiences, the subtle and not-so-subtle differences that make living in a foreign country such a rich and rewarding experience.

On that precipitously steep learning curve, Justi had started to learn the Slovene words she needed, such as *učiteljica* (teacher), *knjižnica* (library) and *zbornica* (staffroom), while I learned food and grocery words such as *kruh* (bread), *mleko* (milk) and *jajca* (eggs). One early mistake I'd made was confusing the Slovene word for jam—*marmalada*—for the orange marmalade we Brits know and love. Justi and I are very partial to our marmalade, so it was quite a disappointment to discover I'd bought a large jar of apricot jam on my first shopping foray. Still, it was tasty jam, and we learned by our mistake.

We'd also learned that, in nearly all Slovene towns and villages, people either lived in quite large detached houses or an apartment block. The houses usually had three storeys and would be home to three generations of a family; the grandparents, parents and their adult offspring would have a separate apartment on each level. We hadn't seen any streets with rows of semi-detached or terraced houses.

Another thing we noticed about Slovene houses was that, like in many alpine countries, the roofs have overhanging eaves that stop the house walls from becoming wet. Even modern homes continue this tradition of architecture, but I suspect its use dates back to when wooden buildings were the norm. It also means you can walk around the outside of the house under protection from the rain, or snow sliding off the roof, while you fetch wood from your stack.

Towards the end of our first week, the rain and fog finally cleared, and a bright autumn sun shone from a cloudless sky. The transformation in the landscape and, not least, our sense of wellbeing, was dramatic. With our moods lifted, we both felt re-energised and ready to discover our new surroundings.

In the afternoons, when school had finished, we began to venture out on short exploratory drives and walks into the verdant countryside. Some of the forested hill roads were fiercely steep and led to tiny hamlets perched on broad ridges cultivated with small fields and orchards. Apple, pear and plum trees hung heavy with their autumn produce, while chickens wandered freely across the road, pecking at the corn dropped from tractors and trailers.

Despite their size, we were happy to discover that many of these little hill villages supported a bar where we would sit outside and enjoy a coffee or cold beer while taking in the panoramic view. It felt wonderful to be able to do this and not have to cover every inch of exposed skin with anti-midge lotion as we'd had to sitting outside the cottage in the Highlands. The lack of strong wind was another revelation. We could open the car door without worrying it would be ripped off its hinges, as was usually the case in the squally Scottish weather.

Some of the steep south-facing slopes had been planted with rows of vines. They were small-scale family-owned vineyards, and each plot had a unique little dwelling and one or two outbuildings. Some of these were built of cut stone and dug partly into the hillside, while others looked more ramshackle, constructed from old wooden planks and corrugated metal. We discovered that the little houses and chalets, called *vikend*—literally because they're used at the weekends—are found throughout the Slovenian countryside. Many Slovene families own a *vikend*, often that they've constructed themselves, which are usually situated in idyllic, off-the-beaten-track locations. Over the years, we've often walked for hours up a seemingly remote forested hillside only to arrive at a *vikend* where a family are enjoying a picnic, their Ford Mondeo parked nearby.

We passed many religious shrines by the side of the roads, each adorned with an intricate wooden carving of a crucified Jesus or the Virgin Mary. On almost every hilltop stood a small church or chapel, just as we'd noticed from the observation tower. Many of them dated from the 18th century with a few being even older; all of them were well maintained. Although Slovenia is predominantly a Roman Catholic country, religion was tolerated rather than encouraged during communist times. Justi had learned from her school colleagues that, even up until the 1980s, teachers and academics would risk being demoted if they were seen to attend religious services.

Jelka had recommended that we try a cup of *vroče čokolada* (hot chocolate) at a bar in the town that had made the drink their speciality. We were keen to try it as we'd been told that it wasn't anything like the usual cup of hot chocolate we Brits drink, which is called *kakav* in Slovene.

The bar was in one of the old neoclassical style buildings, a large room with a high ceiling and Art Deco furnishing. Waiters wound their way expertly between the busy tables, carrying trays of drinks while bar staff stirred pots of melted chocolate behind the long dark wood counter.

Menu boards displayed extensive lists of all the different hot chocolate drinks on offer—milk chocolate, dark chocolate, white chocolate and all with varying percentages of cocoa content. Every drink had a name, and each contained its own unique ingredients such as rum, caramel, coconut, nuts and spices. The melted chocolate is served in big cups and is more like a dessert than a chocolate drink. As it's so thick and creamy, it's best eaten with a spoon. It was chocolate heaven, and the bar was to become one of our favourite haunts on cold winter afternoons.

Chapter 10 Bikes and Vets

Having taken up Dejan's offer to join the local cycling group, I thought I'd better get a few kilometres of riding in my legs before I met them. I hadn't ridden my bike since leaving Scotland, so I expected my first few rides to involve a certain amount of pain and suffering. On our local road map, I'd worked out a route that followed the main valley floor for about twenty kilometres before climbing over a low pass into the next valley that ran parallel. Another small pass would then bring me back into our valley, making a convenient loop of about 45 kilometres, which I thought was adequate for my first outing.

It was quite misty when I set off at about nine in the morning, but I expected it to lift as the forecast was for more sunshine. The main road was quiet as most Slovenes would have been in work for at least two hours by now. I noticed that the few vehicles that passed gave me a wide berth and were patient. I was pleasantly surprised by this, not just because of the poor visibility, but because I'd found it to be just the opposite when driving—Justi and I had both been shocked at the Slovenes' habit of tailgating. Keeping your distance didn't seem to be part of the Slovene Highway Code.

I soon settled into a rhythm, enjoying the cool morning air on my face and the smell of the dewy fields. As I approached my turning point for the first hill pass, a nightmarish vision materialised out of the mist that nearly made me crash.

In the driveway of a farmhouse by the roadside, a family stood gathered around a long table. Two men with bloody knives stood over a plump, naked body covered in blood and lying prostrate on the table, in what looked like an act of cannibalism. Women busily wrapped body parts in bloodstained cloth as small children and dogs ran around the yard playing, seemingly oblivious to the gruesome scene. Another table placed against the wall of the house was piled with bread, cheese and cakes with a bottle of schnapps and upturned glasses on a tray; a macabre celebration.

My initial reaction and instinct was to attempt a record-breaking ascent of the hilly pass. My mind raced as I tried to make sense of the grisly goings-on, and then suddenly I remembered—*koline*! It was the season when Slovene farmers and smallholders dispatched their pig for the table. It was obviously a family affair, though we later learned that the local butcher is sometimes hired to help out too.

Relieved at having found an explanation for the roadside massacre, I began to crank my way up the incline in a series of sweeping bends. The sun had broken through, and the mist had dissipated by the time I reached the top of the pass. Although the view was somewhat limited by the forest, it was still enchanting. I could see the tops of the two highest hills of the area separated by undulating ridges and fertile valleys. The taller of the two peaks, Boč, was a big whaleback of a mountain, while the other, Donačka Gora, had a much more pointed profile.

They looked enticing in the bright sunshine, and I hoped that Justi would feel up to tackling one soon. Although enjoyable, she'd found her first two weeks of teaching utterly exhausting. There was just so much new information to process, not only for her work, but for all the tasks of everyday life in a new country.

As I made my way along the undulating ridge, breaks in the trees revealed small rural settlements. Crude, hand-painted signs outside farmsteads advertised *krompir* (potatoes) and *jabolka* (apples) for sale. I made mental notes of the roadside coffee bars for future rides with Justi.

I enjoyed an exhilarating freewheel into the next valley, which also had a spa town. Huge billboards boasted of outdoor swimming pools, a myriad of different health therapies and locally bottled spa water. Although the holiday season was over, we'd noticed that the local spa towns were offering out-of-season discounts and packages that attracted a fair number of visitors at weekends.

Justi and I had been struck by Slovenia's incredible café culture, and as I cycled through the town, I enjoyed seeing local people sitting outside the bars under sunshades, enjoying coffee, cakes and ice creams. *I could get used to this*, I thought.

I returned home from my ride just before midday and started to prepare some food before Justi arrived. Having begun to adopt Slovene eating times and habits, which are quite different from the ones we were used to in the UK, I knew Justi would only want a very light lunch. The Slovenes don't eat much, if anything, when they first get up in the morning. A Slovene breakfast might consist of a cup of coffee or a fruit juice and maybe a pastry. Most Slovenes find the thought of a typical UK cooked breakfast of bacon, eggs, sausage, toast, etc. quite distasteful.

I suspect this is simply because they rise so early. However, Slovenes have their breakfast in mid-morning in the form of a snack which they call *malica*. Justi would have had her school *malica* at about 10 a.m., but to someone from the UK, *malica* could hardly be described as a snack. It could be meatballs, pasta or cakes, all served in generous portions. The Slovenes eat their main meal of the day (*kosilo*) at about 3 p.m. and have an evening snack called *večerja*. We'd noticed how much the Slovenes liked their salad; every *gostilna* (inn) has a help-yourself salad bar with a big selection from which to fill your bowl. There's always a good choice of homemade dressings to go with it too. In the same way that you would expect to see a lorry driver tucking into a full English at a truck stop in the UK, it isn't unusual to see the Slovene equivalent tucking into a bowl of luscious leafiness in a roadside café bar here.

We'd arranged to take Bryn to a government-registered vet in the afternoon to have a rabies booster and be checked for various fur and skin parasites. This was a legal requirement as we were now outside the EU. After lunch, Justi and I gave him a short walk, pleased that the street guard dogs were no longer so vocal. Maybe they'd just become used to the strange newcomers, or perhaps they weren't so keen to hear the sonic discord of the Dazer again.

Collecting Bryn's veterinary documents from the apartment, I opened the rear of the car, and he jumped in enthusiastically. If he'd known what was coming, he mightn't have been so eager, and with hindsight, we would have driven much further to have him treated by a different vet.

Although Podpetek had a vet whom we'd met and found to be both amiable and helpful, we had to drive quite a distance to see the vet who was specially qualified to deal with animals imported into the country. When we arrived at the surgery, we were a little surprised to see a few empty horseboxes and farm trailers parked up in a big yard outside, and what looked like a row of stables to the rear of the building.

We walked into the empty waiting room and rang a bell on the end of the reception desk. As we waited, we looked at posters and adverts on the walls showing pictures of cattle, pigs and horses, along with detailed enlarged images of all the various parasites that can inflict them, and a small alarm bell sounded in my head. After a few moments, the door to the side of the reception desk opened, and a man put his head out and nodded curtly at us.

'Hello, we have an appointment to see you about our dog,' I said, 'We've recently arrived in Slovenia.'

Justi handed him Bryn's medical documents. He grunted, looked down at Bryn and then brusquely indicated to us to follow him into an examination room. He seemed agitated by our presence, as if he'd drawn the short straw, with Bryn being his forfeit. From the moment we'd seen the posters in the waiting room, we'd begun to deduce that small animals weren't this vet's usual patients. Unfortunately, he only had a few words of English, so it was impossible to try and discuss his aggravations and diffuse the tensions that were steadily rising.

He motioned that we should lift Bryn onto the steel table in the middle of the room then turned his attention to the documents Justi had handed to him. He flicked through the pages irritably. He mimed that we must hold Bryn's head while he shaved the fur off one of his front legs to draw a blood sample. Bryn, who looked worried most of the time, looked even more worried than usual as the vet approached, holding an unnervingly large syringe of the type you'd imagine would be used on a half-tonne ruminant. The vet muttered and grumbled as he failed to find a vein, blood flowing everywhere except into the syringe. After his third attempt, he finally managed to obtain sufficient blood for a lab test. By now, Bryn had given up all hope and lay slumped over Justi's shoulder with a resigned look on his face. But his ordeal was far from over yet.

The vet needed a sample of fur, and using a large pair of tweezers, he started plucking from the soft undercoat on Bryn's back. We tried to comfort our poor dog with soft, reassuring words, but we could see every muscle in his back flinch and twitch in painful spasms as the vet tugged and dragged his fur out. We wanted so much to pick Bryn up and leave this torture chamber, but there was still one more procedure that the vet was required to do by law. He needed to take a dermatological sample—a skin scrape. The vet shaved another area on one of Bryn's legs, and then with a sharp blade, he began scraping off a thin layer of the exposed skin.

During all three procedures, the vet showed no sign whatsoever of kindly attentiveness towards Bryn. He was obviously not well versed in dealing with small animals or pets; in fact, I doubt if he saw any pets at all. His main job was obviously to examine and treat farm livestock, including some that had been imported into the country. As soon as he'd issued us with the necessary certificate to show that Bryn had undergone the procedures, we left as quickly as possible, feeling upset and angry. As I held the door open for Justi and Bryn to make their getaway, I looked back to see the vet mopping up pools of blood from the table.

A lot of dogs would have been unable to control their fear and instincts, which would probably have resulted in the vet having his hand stitched. Bryn always behaved impeccably during visits to the vet, but he'd truly excelled himself on this occasion. On the way home, we stopped at a supermarket to buy him some treats. The thought of him licking his wounds alone in the austere confines of the garage filled us both with sadness.

*****

By 7 a.m. on Sunday morning, I was up and out walking Bryn, who thankfully had quickly recovered from his ordeal, to get back for breakfast before going out again. I'd arranged to meet Dejan and his cycling friends to join them for a two-hour ride. Dejan and two other cyclists were already waiting outside the post office building on one side of the town square. He introduced his friends, who looked disconcertingly fitter and younger than me, and said that they expected another four or five cyclists to arrive shortly.

As we chatted, my attention was drawn to a man standing on the post office steps, leaning into a rusty old pram that was adorned with tattered flags and bunting. He was wearing a scruffy-looking khaki military uniform and a metal infantry helmet. He lifted cardboard placards from the pram and placed them against the post office wall.

One or two were in English and read 'No to NATO!' and 'Down with America and Bush!' He then picked up a Slovene flag on a pole and started to parade, marching back and forth along the top of the office steps while singing and smiling happily at passers-by. He had a friendly congeniality about him that assuaged the sense that he could be threatening in any way.

'Who's that?' I asked Dejan.

'Oh, he's just a madman. Ignore him. He's a crazy old communist, and he does this every weekend.'

The few Slovenes we'd spoken to regarding Slovenia's place in the world of politics and allegiances had all been upbeat about the country's forthcoming accession to the EU. However, there was less enthusiasm for joining NATO, and on the odd occasion we'd seen graffiti since being here, it was in the form of anti-NATO slogans.

The rest of the cyclists arrived, and I was relieved to see that two of them were quite a bit older than the rest of the group, so, hopefully, the pace wouldn't be too high. As we readied to set off, I waved to the man on the post office steps. He waved back, smiling, then stood smartly to attention and saluted before making a sharp about-turn and continuing with his one-man demonstration.

As we rode single file, our little peloton carefully negotiated the main road out of town before turning off onto a quiet lane. Dejan dropped back and rode alongside me as we started up a steep incline. He was obviously fitter than me and chatted easily without sounding out of breath. He asked me about cycling in Scotland and what I thought about the Slovene roads while I wheezed out answers economically, trying to divert all available oxygen to my leg muscles.

The younger riders moved to the front and started to pull away up the hill. The two older cyclists were pedalling at a more leisurely pace behind us. They were friends who'd both recently retired from work and were keen to ride as much as possible. One of them had bought himself a new, state-of-the-art carbon race bike from Italy for his retirement. Although we couldn't communicate with language, they seemed pleased at the opportunity to show off their local countryside to the 'English'.

We regrouped at the top of the hill and continued along a relatively level scenic road with small fields and vineyards on either side. As we passed one of the fields, I heard a melodic knocking sound and glanced over my shoulder to see what it was.

'*Klopotec*!' shouted one of the older cyclists, smiling, having noticed my interest in locating the source of the mesmerising sound. He pointed towards the centre of the field where a large pole stood. It supported what looked like a small wooden windmill. Instead of cloth sails, the device had angled blades of wood that were nailed to an axle. As the breeze blew, the blades spun, and on each rotation, they struck a piece of wood fixed to the pole. It was a Slovene bird-scarer, and it produced a noise that can best be described as a pleasing, woody 'klop' sound. When the wind picked up, the blades spun faster, and it made a sound that reminded me of the wooden rattles that used to be heard at football matches. This was the first day since we'd been in Slovenia that I'd noticed any wind, so the numerous *klopotec* had been silent. There were scarecrows in most fields too, which stood in for the *klopotec* on windless days.

The route we cycled was very enjoyable; the roads were quiet and the scenery superb. Every so often, the more competitive riders in the group would pull away to reach the top of an incline first, or sprint to reach a road sign as though it was a stage finish in a race. We followed the road along the top of a forested ridge with steep-sided valleys on either side, and I guessed that we were very close to the border with Croatia. Looking down through a break in the trees, I could see a small settlement on the valley floor.

'*Ustaše*!' scoffed one of the group riding next to me, nodding his head towards the houses below. The *Ustaše* were a Croatian fascist militia group responsible for the deaths of many Yugoslavs, including large numbers of Slovenes, during WW2. It seemed that old grievances had been passed on and not yet forgotten.

Returning to the town centre, I left my new cycling friends after making arrangements to meet again for a mid-week ride after work. It had been an enjoyable and informative trip, and I was already looking forward to the next one, though I realised that, with winter on the horizon, the cycling season in Slovenia would soon be over.

Chapter 11 Culture Clash

It was mid-October, and although we were beginning to feel more comfortable in our new surroundings, there was still a great deal to learn regarding the language and traditions of Slovenia. One aspect of Slovene culture seemed particularly alien to us—staring. In Britain, we're taught from early childhood that it's rude to stare. It's something that most Brits accept and never question. It's so deep in our culture that to stare at a fellow Brit makes them feel uncomfortable, and in certain situations, it can result in violent retaliation.

That may sound disproportionate for something as harmless as looking in the 'wrong' direction, but I can attest to hearing the threatening, knee-trembling accusation—'Who you lookin' at, eh?' On that particular occasion, the question was coming from a psychopathic-looking skinhead who seemed intent on finding a bit of 'bovver' on the top deck of a nearly empty last bus on my way home from a city-centre pub. Luckily, though, as I desperately tried to avoid any more eye contact and assess my get-out-of-this-one options, he stumbled down the stairs for his fast-approaching stop.

This type of scenario played out a few more times in my younger adult years and usually involved an innocent stare or absent-minded glance at someone during an alcohol-infused night out in my home city. Making any attempt to answer the 'Who you lookin' at?' question is unlikely to defuse the situation, especially if you answer, 'Nobody,' as I once did. Violence was avoided on that occasion too, but only after I'd managed to 'do a Linford Christie' and unofficially broken the 100-metre sprint record.

Staring or looking at a stranger in Slovenia, or, indeed, in most mainland European countries, is very unlikely to be considered an act of provocation or a challenge to your masculinity. During our first few weeks in Slovenia, we felt uncomfortable when walking Bryn through the neighbourhood. Despite our enthusiastic smiling and nodding, people in their gardens would stop digging or hanging out their washing and stare as we passed by. I suspect this initial look of suspicion was simply because we were living in a part of the town that strangers or tourists wouldn't usually visit. The cool response was only temporary, and after about three weeks, when it was becoming evident that we weren't on holiday, our friendly '*Dober dan*' (Good day) was being warmly reciprocated.

Visitors find that generally everywhere they go in Slovenia, they will be greeted with '*Dober dan*', a friendly smile and a healthy amount of eye contact.

After many years now living in Slovenia, I must confess to a mischievous game that Justi and I play while sitting at a café in tourist locations—Spot the Brit. We can spot Brits at 100 metres. It's not difficult for a whole number of reasons, but one of the ultimate giveaways is that they're usually the ones who avoid eye contact at all costs when they pass by.

Although it probably can't be classed as a cultural difference, British people visiting Slovenia will often be surprised at how careful and serious the Slovenes are when it comes to jaywalking and the Green Cross Code. If you find yourself standing at traffic lights in Slovenia with other pedestrians, do not cross until the little green man gives the thumbs-up, unless you wish to endure scolding looks or even a little verbal admonishment. It may be the quietest of roads where you can see clearly in both directions along the empty lanes for a kilometre each way, but everyone will be standing stock still and waiting for the green light. It's hard to shed the years of sturrying (an apt word used to describe that quick dash across the road between traffic—see the priceless book *The Meaning of Liff* by Douglas Adams & John Lloyd) if you come from the UK.

Twice during our early days in Slovenia, Justi had been reprimanded for crossing the road on a red light on her way to school, even though there wasn't any traffic in sight. Embarrassingly, it was the same finger-wagging police officer who stopped her on both occasions. It's interesting to note that, despite being a member of the Vienna Convention on Road Traffic, the UK is the only country that doesn't enforce the convention's laws when it comes to jaywalking. The British Highway Code allows the pedestrian to make their own judgement when it comes to crossing the road.

During the second week of her new teaching job, Justi had attended an induction course where she met the other foreign language assistants who had newly joined the scheme. The assistant working at the Podpetek secondary school was an American called Jake who lent Justi an informative book, illustrated with hilarious cartoons, about the cultural differences between Slovenia and Britain. One of the things it mentioned was how often Brits are disturbed by the open and direct eye contact which is a normal part of Slovene culture. What a relief. We no longer felt like goldfish in a bowl.

Jake was in his mid-30s and from California. He was a tall, youthful-looking guy with a huge friendly smile and a thick mop of sun-bleached hair. It would be easy to imagine Jake casually strolling down the street in Podpetek with a surfboard under his arm, even though the sea is several hours' drive away. He had an easy, laid-back, son-of-a-beach attitude, but he also managed to exhibit a passionate enthusiasm for most things in life.

Jake had met Mateja, his Slovene wife, while she was on a working holiday in California on an organic farm. After marrying and living in the USA for five years, Mateja had become desperately homesick and persuaded Jake to move to Slovenia. It didn't take him long to fall in love with the country, and they quickly settled into the lifestyle and made plans to raise a family.

The four of us soon became good friends, sharing our everyday experiences over a meal or a drink and going for walks together in the surrounding hills. It was lovely to chat and unwind with Jake and Mateja after days spent struggling to understand the complex grammar and alien sounds of the Slovene language.

We often joked about the subtle and not-so-subtle differences between American English and British English which occasionally resulted in farcical misunderstandings. One afternoon, Justi and I agreed how nice it would be to see Jake and Mateja, so I picked up the phone to invite them around for the evening.

'Hi, Jake, it's Roy.'

'Hey, Roy, how ya doing buddy?' replied Jake in his eager, yet somehow mellow, Californian drawl.

'Jake, would you and Mateja like to come to ours for some nosh?'

'Oh, yeah, faaantaaastic. We'd love to,' came the answer on a wave of unadulterated enthusiasm.

'OK, Jake, see you in about an hour.'

Five minutes later, the phone rang.

'Hey, Roy.' It was Jake, his voice sounding slightly sheepish.

'Oh, hi, Jake, is anything wrong?'

'Er, no, nothing wrong, but what exactly is nosh?'[2]

*****

By the end of October, our remaining funds were reaching a critical point. Because Justi had started her job towards the end of September, her first wage had been barely a third of a full month's salary. We still had about £200 of our original savings left, so by tightening our belts, we were hoping to make it through till the second week in November, when she would receive a full salary. Then a small financial bombshell landed when Jelka casually asked us if we'd bought our winter tyres yet.

'Winter tyres?' we replied in unison, with undisguised alarm in our voices.

'Yes, it's the law in Slovenia. Your car must be equipped with a set of winter tyres between November 15th and March 15th.'

This was going to erase the rest of our savings in one rubbery stroke, and we'd have to poke a few extra notches in our already tightly drawn belts. Winter tyres brought a crazy Mad Max world to mind in my overindulgent imagination. I imagined them to be impaled with shiny metal studs or fiendish nails like those used on ice speedway bikes. In reality, they look just like standard summer tyres, except that the tread is a little deeper, and the rubber compound is better formulated to deal with cold temperatures. After being tipped off as to the best value local garage, a set of tyres was fitted to the Chariot, and we were legally prepared for the winter season. Still, as I handed over the last of our savings to the mechanic, I felt a little cheated that the tyres weren't fitted with three-inch-long, tungsten-tipped titanium spikes.

*****

---

[2] A colloquial British word for food.

Although Justi and I had fallen into our new routines, I couldn't help but feel uncomfortable about my new role as a house husband. I'd been used to us both going out to work, and I felt that my daily tasks were no longer as relevant or equal to Justi's employment. Justi, on the other hand, was far happier with the arrangement. She knew that Bryn had a lot of company, and she didn't have to worry about the domestic issues of life, such as shopping and cooking, when working in such a new environment was difficult enough. While I struggled with my conscience and British protestant work ethic, Justi enjoyed and appreciated the supportive role that I'd taken on.

I considered making some enquiries with our Slovene friends as to the possibility of working self-employed as a gardener, as I had done in the Highlands.

'I really feel I should contribute financially,' I told Justi.

'It would be impossible for you to get a work permit, and the language and meagre pay mean it's not a worthwhile option,' she pointed out.

'I know you're right.' I sighed.

'Look, if the boot was on the other foot and our roles were reversed, no one, including me, would think there was anything unusual about our circumstances,' she said with genuine truth and tenderness. I had to agree with her, but it still left me feeling troubled and anxious, not least for our very fragile financial situation.

As I became a regular on the local cycle club rides, I overheard my name being mentioned amid some mirth and furtive chuckling at a Sunday meet. I recognised the word for slippers—*copata*—in the same sentence as my name, so I asked Dejan what the joke was about.

'Oh, they're only having a little fun at your expense. It's nothing; they are just jealous.'

He went on to explain that a *copata* man was someone who spent lots of time at home and was subjugated by his wife to do all the domestic chores. This attempt to strike a gentle blow to my masculinity had less of an effect than it would have had the previous month, as I was becoming more aware how Justi and I were able to function happily as a pair in our new country. Our different roles of support complemented and helped each other deal with all the new challenges we faced. Although we didn't have much money, we'd never been great spenders and had decided early on in our lives that collecting memories was far more fun than collecting 'things'. Relatively speaking, we didn't have much material 'stuff', but we both considered our lives to be very rich.

A week or so later, after another club meet, one of the more macho team members—who was probably the instigator of the slipper-man comments—chatted with me after the ride. Boštjan worked on a production line in a busy local engineering factory and was passionate about his cycling. We talked for a while about bikes and what it was like to cycle in the UK. Just before we left for home, he said, 'Roy, I wish I had a lifestyle like yours. I'm not happy in my work, and I wish I could spend more time with my family.'

His voice sounded wistful and contemplative. Maybe he thought being a slipper man wasn't such a bad thing after all.

*****

My earlier concerns about having to leave the country regularly to renew a tourist visa hadn't materialised. Slovenia was already gearing up for EU membership, and we found that the authorities were quite relaxed when it came to EU citizens visiting their country, even for extended periods. It was with a light heart that, towards the end of November, we found ourselves chugging our way north over the border to Austria in the Great White Chariot. We'd arranged to meet Justi's sister Cath with Vic and Betty at Graz airport. Cath was making good on her promise to visit us as soon as we were settled in Slovenia.

Although we had a spare room for Betty, Rozalija was still adamant that we had to pay extra rent for any visitors to our apartment, so they'd all booked themselves into one of the big spa hotels near the old square. It was lovely to see them, but any hopes we had of showing them around the beautiful Slovene countryside in bright sunshine were scuppered by an unusual forecast of fog and low cloud for the entire week. Still, we enjoyed a few short walks and visited some of our favourite cafés and bars with the fog adding atmosphere and ambience to the neoclassical spa buildings. The abnormal, dank weather also added a moody aura to some of the more modern spa hotels and health clinics. Although most had been recently renovated, their original stark communist architecture seemed highlighted in the swirling mists of greyness.

With Cath and Vic, we swam in one of the spa swimming pools in the evenings, and although it had the look and feel of a utilitarian health facility, it had a lot of modern technical features such as varying temperature zones, whirlpools and Jacuzzis. It was also possible to swim under a barrier that gave access to an outdoor section of the pool. It was lovely to swim outside and experience the contrast of being in warm water as the steam rose through the cold and foggy night air.

With help from one of our Slovene friends, we arranged a tour of the local glass factory. Cath jumped at the chance to have a go at glass blowing, but we were all concerned and a bit shocked that she wasn't offered any protective clothing. However, she survived her attempt and produced a very passable bowl of glass heated to a blistering yellow temperature.

Despite the lack of any views due to the fog, Cath and Vic enjoyed the Slovene cuisine and swimming in the spa pools. When we took them back to the airport, the sun blazed from an azure sky over the city of Graz, and we spent a happy few hours together, wandering around the beautiful old town centre.

It was another moment of sad departure, but this time, Betty seemed satisfied knowing that her daughter was safe and well in a beautiful country called Slovenia—not Slovakia.

It had been challenging to communicate easily with our families in the first few weeks after we arrived. Neither Justi nor I owned mobile phones, and we had to rely on the public payphones located in the town centre. Feeding our limited tolars into the phone coin boxes on dark, rain-soaked evenings sometimes made our loved ones seem even further away. It was on one such evening while talking to my folks that my dad mentioned that we needed to check our bank account as we could expect a gift for both our birthdays. He went on to explain that they'd transferred some money that was to be used for two mobile phones. It was a generous gift that made our lives so much easier for many years to come, and both my dad and Betty also bought mobile phones so we could send text messages and be in immediate contact.

So far, our dreams of visiting the Julian Alps with any regularity had been thwarted by the travelling distance, combined with our lack of sufficient time and money. For the moment, we had to be satisfied with climbing the two highest local hills and several smaller ones.

We enjoyed every minute walking on the forested paths and visiting the mountain huts, called *dom* or *koča*. The outdoor life has always been an important part of Slovene culture, and waymarked walking trails criss-cross the whole countryside. In the higher, steeper mountains, the routes are protected with a plethora of steel cables, metal pegs and rungs to make them accessible to as many people as possible.

With our tentative plans to walk in the Julian Alps and, hopefully, climb Triglav on hold, another group of hills had caught our attention a short distance to the north—the Pohorje Mountains, close to the city of Maribor. We could reach the foot of these gentle, tree-covered hills after a 45-minute drive and enjoy long treks through the sweet-smelling pine forests. On the high, undulating plateaus, we walked through open, grassy glades where we would sometimes find metal-framed viewing platforms similar to the one we'd found in Podpetek, only higher. The views above the treetops were extensive. We could look north into the rolling Austrian countryside with its meandering rivers and sapphire blue lakes, but what caught our eye most on the first occasion we climbed a tower was the view to the west. It was in that direction that we saw silhouetted jagged mountains—first the Kamnik-Savinja Alps, then beyond, Triglav and the Julian Alps, looking distant yet serenely majestic in the setting sun of an early winter's evening. It was our first view of the Julian Alps, and it made us even more determined to visit them at the first opportunity.

As we descended the path back down to our car that evening, Justi noticed that much of what appeared to be grass in the glades and along the path edges was composed of many different types of leaves. They were the leaves of alpine flowers and meadow plants, and we could only imagine the colourful splendour that awaited us on our springtime walking adventures.

Chapter 12 A White Christmas

Ever since we'd arrived in Podpetek, we'd kept our ears open and asked Slovene friends to tell us about any apartments that might become available to rent. We'd given our notice to Rozalija and Marko almost as soon as we'd moved in. Their apartment was spacious and modern, but there were several issues regarding our tenancy that had made us unhappy. Although we were on friendly terms, it was clear that the tenant relationship with our landlords wasn't entirely compatible, and most of all we wanted Bryn to be with us indoors during the coming winter evenings. So we were delighted when Jelka told us that an apartment was available and that Bryn would be allowed in.

It was just before Christmas when we went to view the ground floor apartment in a house on a residential street not far away from the school. The owners of the house, Bojana and Igor, greeted us warmly and invited us into a brightly tiled hallway and through to a big living room with a high ceiling. They were retired caterers who lived upstairs, and the vacant apartment had been their daughter's, who was now at university and living in Ljubljana.

Bojana was a big lady with a head of the bright copper-coloured hair that's very popular with Slovene women. She was the type of woman who imbued a sense of warmth and motherliness and made you think of your favourite aunt. She was full of playful humour and self-parody, but it was also easy to sense that she was someone not to be crossed, being fair yet firm.

Igor was a tall, slim, balding man with a quiet, friendly manner and a thoughtful facial expression. He spoke a reasonable amount of English in a slow, deliberate way, but he also had a sharp sense of wit and satire about him. Bojana had only a handful of English words, and with our very rudimentary Slovene skills, I wondered how we would manage to negotiate our way through any tenancy agreement details.

However, Jelka had told us that all the official documents had been dealt with and that we needn't have any concerns about unfavourable rules and conditions. We just needed to sign the papers if we were happy with the apartment.

Despite her lack of English, Bojana was the most communicative person we'd ever met, and she didn't seem in the least perturbed that we couldn't speak Slovene. After a brief conversation between Igor and Bojana, he disappeared upstairs while Bojana showed us around the rest of the apartment. It was smaller than Rozalija's, but it was much more comfortable and had a homely and cosy feel.

As she was proudly showing us the fully equipped kitchen, we heard a clink of glasses and bottles as Igor arrived back from upstairs.

'Come,' said Bojana, and she ushered us back into the living room where Igor was opening a bottle of schnapps and filling a round of glasses; on the table lay the tenancy documents. After a toast of '*Nazdravje!*' '*Prost!*' and 'Cheers!' we brought up the subject of Bryn.

'Can we bring our dog into the apartment?' asked Justi tentatively.

There was a brief pause as Bojana appeared not to understand, and Igor's expression looked especially thoughtful.

'Our *pes*?' Justi went on as she tried a bit of Sloglish—our mixture of languages.

Just as Igor started to translate, Bojana grasped the question and replied excitedly, 'Ya, ya, bring dog, bring dog!'

I left Justi getting to know our new friends and went to fetch Bryn from the Chariot. He didn't hesitate to make his way inside the house and obviously sensed that his three-month solitary confinement in the garage might be coming to an end.

'Come on, Bryn, come here and lie down,' said Justi, eager that Bryn shouldn't show too much boisterous enthusiasm to our hosts. She needn't have worried, though, as Bojana and Igor clearly wanted to make a big fuss of him.

'Breen, Breen!' cried Bojana, almost in tears. She was obviously both pleased and upset at meeting Bryn, and it took us by surprise. We couldn't understand what would cause such an outburst and mix of emotions. As she patted and stroked our slightly bemused collie, Igor explained that their much-loved dog had recently died, and its name had been Brin, which means juniper in Slovene. Although both our dogs' names had different meanings, we were amazed at this extraordinary coincidence. It felt like a sign that we'd finally found the right apartment.

In the 30 minutes or so of our first meeting, we felt we'd made friends with our hosts. Bryn certainly had, especially when Bojana made an excursion upstairs to her kitchen and returned with a plate of cooked chicken for him. With his eyes almost popping out of his head and his chops drooling, Christmas had arrived a week early for Bryn. Justi and I didn't need any further discussion; we'd already decided that we were moving into Bojana and Igor's apartment, and signing the tenancy papers was just a legal formality.

The very next day saw us moving our belongings across town and settling into our new place. It was particularly good to be able to put Bryn's basket in the corner of the living room and have him with us again. Bojana came down to see how we were getting on and brought another choice piece of cooked meat for Bryn that looked delicious. Smiling, Justi and I exchanged a wicked glance—Bryn might have to share some of his tasty treats with his pack mates. Bojana also kindly handed us a box of Christmas decorations. 'For apartment,' she said.

*****

Justi had completed her first term, and the school were having their annual Christmas party meal. The principal, who'd made a point of involving me in extra-curricular school activities since we'd arrived in Podpetek, had also thoughtfully invited me along for the staff meal. There was lots of delicious Slovene food to try, but one of the simplest items on the menu immediately became one of our favourite staples and still is to this day. *Pražen krompir* might be recognised merely as mashed potato by most of us Brits, but there's a bit more to it than that. The potatoes are cooked and partly mashed then lightly fried with onions in lard and seasoned with black pepper. Chives are often added during cooking, or maybe even a little garlic, depending on your taste. We now prefer to fry it lightly in butter, but either way, it's a simple and tasty side dish for many meals.

Sašo, a big affable guy who managed the school sports hall, was sitting opposite us. We'd met him not long after Justi had begun her job, when we were invited by some of her colleagues, including Sašo, for a meal at a local *gostilna*. This soon turned into a regular Friday lunchtime event that we always looked forward to. On the night of the Christmas party, Sašo seemed determined to get the Englishman drunk and introduced me to one after another 'best Slovene vine'. I'm certainly no wine expert, but Slovenian wines are probably one of the most underrated products in Europe. They're still not very well known outside the country, and I suspect this is simply because the amounts produced aren't enough for serious export. The Slovenes are very proud of their wines, and rightly so, in my opinion.

Another Slovene teacher colleague at the party, and another Friday lunchtime friend, was Kasija. Soon due to retire from her lifelong job as a maths teacher, she was an extraordinary lady whom we liked instantly. She was slightly eccentric and certainly didn't fit the image of the usual smartly dressed, professional-looking Slovene school teacher. She always wore a khaki hunter's jacket with a myriad of small pockets; she said it saved her carrying a handbag. Right from the beginning, she was eager to meet Justi and me because she'd heard that we'd lived in the Scottish Highlands, and it seemed she had an interest in the area.

During our very first conversation, I was recommending the beauties of a particularly remote Highland glen when Kasija stopped me in mid-flow.

'Has Mr Fraser fixed the fence near the head of the glen yet?' she asked.

'What? You've *been* to the glen? You mean you really know it?'

It turned out that Kasija had been visiting the Scottish Highlands in every summer school holiday for the last 35 years. She must have spent over four years in total wandering among the hills and glens of her beloved Highlands, gaining an intimate knowledge of the Scottish landscape and weather. She'd also made many Scottish friends over the years, and Mr Fraser, an elderly worker on a remote Highland estate, was one of them.

I'd lived and worked for twelve years in the Highlands and prided myself on my knowledge of the Scottish mountains and coastal areas, particularly in the west. Kasija put my knowledge to the test, and she could often describe some of the remote wild glens with far more intimacy and detail than I could recall. It became a Friday lunchtime game to find somewhere in the Highlands that Kasija hadn't visited.

She eagerly told us of her longing to spend even more time in Scotland when she retired, but sadly, her plans were to prove short-lived. We were all devastated when she succumbed to cancer only a few years later.

During the Christmas holiday, we awoke one morning to an eerie silence and an intuitive feeling that something was different outside. We heard a car driving slowly past the house, but its engine noise sounded peculiarly muffled and quiet.

It was still dark as I opened the roller shutters on our bedroom window and looked out at a white world of deep soft snow. Light feathery flakes were falling in a continuous dense curtain, almost blotting out the yellow glow of the streetlamps.

'What's it like out there?' Justi asked, propping herself up in bed.

'Well, they'll be happy at the local ski slope,' I replied, grinning over my shoulder at her, pleased that our first winter in Slovenia looked set to be a spectacularly white one.

By midday, the snowfall had eased, and we were both anxious to get out and discover our new wintry environment.

'Let's put our cross-country skis in the Chariot and head out to that big open plain to the east,' I suggested. 'It will be a good chance to test our winter tyres too.'

The Chariot, parked in the drive, was almost invisible under its thick blanket of snow. We carefully cleared the snow off and heaped it into the garden using a large plastic snow shovel that Igor had left against the wall of the house. Looking down the street, it seemed that everyone owned one of these useful shovels, and we waved to the neighbour opposite who was out clearing his driveway. He looked to be in his late 60s, and I'd seen Igor and him talking and laughing together. He waved us to come over to him, but before we got there, he'd disappeared through a door at the rear of his garage. We stood outside in the driveway, not sure quite what to do next.

In less than a minute, the door was flung open wide, and our neighbour beckoned us inside. He produced a tray with a bottle of schnapps and glasses and started filling them. With lots of smiles and apologies that involved me pointing at an imaginary watch on my wrist and miming driving the car, we managed to extricate ourselves from another boozy welcoming session after only one glass.

As our faces became better known, it seemed that the local people genuinely wanted to welcome us to their town and neighbourhood. These kind gestures always touched us, but they often involved knocking back several shots of schnapps, most of which were homemade and usually very strong. The strongest ones are typically made from plums or pears, while some of the less potent, and to us nicer-tasting, were made from diverse ingredients such as pine needles, honey and blueberries.

Getting in the car, we made our way tentatively along main roads that had been completely cleared of snow, and we saw several snowploughs spraying huge white waves as they worked their way down minor lanes. We noticed a few tractors that were also fitted with a plough attachment and learned later that, in each village, local farmers were paid to clear the more remote hill roads to get adults to work and children to school on time. No amount of snow seemed to have any effect on the everyday lives of the Slovenes who went about their business unaffected by the seasonal weather. Having winter tyres and knowing that everyone else had them too made driving easy in conditions that would cause motoring mayhem in Britain.

Compared to the UK, the seasons are more clearly defined in Slovenia, and it probably wouldn't make financial sense to have everyone fit winter tyres in Britain for the amount of time they'd be needed. Still, it only takes a couple of days of severe winter weather to witness the media reporting on the billions of pounds lost to the UK economy due to people not being able to get to work. Maybe it would be better if, instead of driving in dangerous conditions, we humans accepted the vagaries of the winter season and enjoyed sledging, skiing and ice skating.

As we drove further east, we left the little rolling hills behind and found ourselves looking out across flat snow-covered fields that stretched to a hazy, milky horizon. Gusts of wind formed twisting dervishes of snow that sped spiralling across the chilly expanse. It was atmospheric and reminded me of winter scenes from well-known and obscure films such as *Doctor Zhivago* and *Dersu Uzala*.

We pulled off the road at a suitable spot and shared a flask of tea and a piece of homemade Christmas cake that Betty had brought over in November. Feeling fortified, we got our skis out and made several circuits of a large field, battling into the strong icy blasts with heads down. When we'd finally had enough, the light was beginning to fade, and we grinned at each other's frosty face, our eyebrows and hats decorated with ice. It was a rewarding introduction to our first outdoor Slovene winter day, and we looked forward to many more.

*****

On the evening of the last day of what had been an exciting year for us, Justi and I decided to make our way up the local hill and climb the viewing tower. We reckoned it would be an ideal spot to see the fireworks going off in the town and local villages. We had the tower to ourselves; no one else seemed foolhardy enough to plough their way up through the snow to stand on the swaying metal tower in minus five degrees.

As midnight approached, a few standard fireworks started lighting up the sky. Above the sound of rockets rocketing by and bangers banging, we heard, and I swear felt, an almighty CRUMP! Then another, slightly more distant, followed by more—one or two on the Croatian side of the border. It brought to mind the sound of big military guns or tanks you'd expect to hear when the red flag is flying on Salisbury Plain in the UK.

On the dot of midnight, a huge eruption of fireworks exploded into the cold night air, complimented by one or two more alarming 'crumps', and we hugged each other, wondering what the next year would bring and where we would be to celebrate the following New Year.

The next day, Jake and Mateja enlightened us as to the heavy explosive sounds we'd heard.

'Oh, that's just the local farmers with their homemade bombs,' Mateja explained. 'They make their own spectacular "fireworks" using up their old fertilisers and weed killers and loading them into a big metal drum or bin.'

It sounded a dangerous way to see in the New Year, but we didn't hear or see any news reports that told of recent Slavic farmer fatalities.

Chapter 13 Under Our Skin

It had been a white winter so far, even in the east of Slovenia which doesn't always get as much snow as the northern, more mountainous parts of the country. Many small towns in Slovenia have a ski slope, with usually just a single tow which may be a simple rope pulley. Podpetek was no exception, and most evenings, it was well used; when the locals had finished work, they enjoyed themselves by sharpening up their considerable skills on the piste beneath the bright spotlights.

We've heard it said that one in three Slovenes ski, and I'm sure it's true. I'd taught myself to ski when I was 35 as a condition to dating Justi, who was already a competent skier. Although I'd quickly learned to negotiate my way down the piste safely, it seemed I had an awful lot to learn as we watched Slovene kids as young as four or five making their way expertly down the slope. It was both wonderful and humbling.

Justi had learned that her school would be closing in mid-February for the Slovene winter holiday, a week-long break that allows Slovenes to get out and enjoy the snow with their families and friends. In order to avoid the ski resorts becoming overwhelmed, the Ministry of Education closes all the schools in the two largest cities, Ljubljana and Maribor, for one week, then the rest of the country's schools for the following week. What a great idea, we thought.

As we were now settled in our new apartment with a lower monthly rent and had paid for our winter tyres, we didn't feel quite so anxious about our finances. Excited, we made a plan to drive across the country to the ski resort of Kranjska Gora in the north-west corner of Slovenia and see the Julian Alps up close. Justi phoned the Kranjska Gora tourist office to see what accommodation was available during the holiday week, and a friendly, helpful-sounding man responded.

'The holiday week won't be a problem,' he assured Justi.

'Accommodation is plentiful. You can just turn up without making a booking.'

'We also have a dog; will that be a problem?' Justi went on.

'No, it won't be a problem. Most hotels and guesthouses are happy to take pets,' the man told her, sounding relaxed and upbeat.

A small alarm bell still sounded in Justi's head, and his words were unable to silence it. She felt a twinge of doubt and scepticism but, with some reluctance, accepted his local knowledge and advice.

The evening before our holiday, we loaded the Chariot with our skis and checked our road atlas to plot our drive across the country to take in one or two places of interest that we'd read about in our *Lonely Planet* guide. In early 2003, the Slovene motorway system was still being developed, so the route was slow and arduous at times as the road meandered through the undulating rural countryside. We drove through the region known as Styria, where we were surprised to see vast areas of land used to grow high-quality hops. Last year's hop plants appeared dry and lifeless in the cold winter air, tied to kilometres of wire that was strung between tall wooden stakes braced at angles to support the weight of the crop.

One of the places we stopped at was Kamnik, an ancient town with two castles and a Franciscan monastery. It was about the halfway point on our journey and offered a stunning backdrop of the Kamnik-Savinja Alps.

After a walk up to one of the ruined castles that gave us superb views of the hills, we felt it was time for a coffee break. We chose a cosy-looking café on the edge of the old square and claimed a seat near the window so that we could enjoy a bit of people-watching. We weren't disappointed, as no sooner had we sat down than the large wooden doors of a medieval building in the square were flung open and people poured out into the street. Several were dressed in brightly coloured traditional Slovene clothing, and the atmosphere was one of jovial celebration.

A bride and groom emerged smiling from the building, and a man with an accordion started up a lively polka. He was soon joined by other members of his troupe with bugles, clarinets and a deep, booming tuba, as everyone sauntered happily along together taking up the whole width of the road.

'*Dober dan.*'

The waiter had arrived to take our order, and we turned our gaze from the colourful wedding spectacle to be faced with a thin middle-aged man whose serious demeanour was compromised by an extraordinary moustache.

'Er...*dober dan*,' I replied, trying hard to make eye contact but distracted by what looked like a large edible dormouse attached to his upper lip.

'Vot vould you like?' he asked, instantly detecting my English accent and looking resigned to be meeting yet another customer who was unappreciative of his facial coiffure.

As he went to fetch our coffee and cake, we giggled.

'I wonder if his furry friend detaches itself at night,' Justi speculated. 'Maybe it leads an independent, nocturnal existence all of its own.'

'Well, it doesn't look as serious as its owner,' I replied. 'It's not difficult to imagine it scurrying about the medieval streets of Kamnik after dark, looking for some discarded *potica*[3] cake or even a potential mate.'

We continued on our way, heading west on a rough main road which passed across a broad open plain with the Karavanke hills to our right and a tantalising view of a jagged mountain range ahead in the distance—the Julian Alps.

A section of motorway that was completed took us past Jesenice, a long narrow town that lies at the entrance to the upper Sava Valley, with the Karavanke hills to the north, bordering Austria, and a high plateau called Mežakla to the south. Jesenice owes its existence to the rich iron deposits found in the Karavanke mountains, and a huge ugly steel factory sprawls along its eastern end. High-rise apartment blocks, built in the 1970s to house thousands of steelworkers, dominate the central part of the town.

'What an awful-looking place,' commented Justi.

From our view on the elevated bypass, the town looked grim, and we could never have imagined how significant a place it was to become in our lives.

Just before the motorway disappeared into the long Karavanke

---

[3] A traditional Slovene rolled sponge cake. As every Slovene will tell you, their mother makes the best version.

tunnel that leads through the mountains into Austria, we turned off, following the sign for Kranjska Gora. We grinned excitedly as massive snow-covered hillsides rose to the right side of the valley, and we gasped at the stark beauty of Triglav and the Julian Alps to our left as we passed between the pretty alpine villages of Dovje and Mojstrana. We crossed a bridge over the sparkling Sava River, where the incredible pointed spire of a mountain called Špik took our breath away as it stood directly ahead, sheathed in its glistening winter coat of snow and ice.

After the relatively flat stretches of our journey, I was now struggling to keep my eyes and concentration on the road. In another few kilometres, we reached the sign welcoming us to Kranjska Gora and turned off the main road into the town. Justi squealed with delight as she got her first view of the ski slopes below the impressive mountainous backdrop behind the town. It was busy, and people wandered awkwardly along the centre of the road in their ski boots, seemingly oblivious to drivers like us searching earnestly to find a parking place. After passing through the town, unable to park and making a long loop back along the main road, we finally succeeded in finding a place for the Great White Chariot a little outside the main centre.

As it was now late in the afternoon, we decided first to find the tourist information office and, hopefully, a room for the week. The office was packed with skiers and day-trippers, and it was apparent that we would have to wait a while before we would get to see anyone. The floor was wet and muddy as people clunked about in their ski boots, and an atmosphere of frustration and impatience hung heavy in the muggy air of the small overcrowded room. Voices seemed to be raised, and once or twice, people stomped past us out through the door, muttering; it was clear they weren't happy with the information on offer.

We finally made our way to the front of the desk where a cross man looked up at us from his office chair and waited for our questions. He looked frazzled as beads of sweat stood proud on his balding head and trickled down the sides of his plump, flushed face. A lady member of staff sat to his left, and she seemed to be dealing with the busy situation in a calmer manner.

Justi decided that this was the man she must have spoken to the previous week.

'Hi, I'm Justi. I phoned you last week about accommodation.'

'What?' he replied, in a robotic, monotone voice and with a blank expression.

'We need a room for two, and we have our dog with us. You said it wouldn't be a problem if we just turned up, so here we are.'

'Accommodation is a problem,' he said, sounding exasperated.

'Well, you told me it wouldn't be a problem and that—'

'Look, lady, it's a national holiday here in Slovenia,' he cut in loudly and sharply, the veins on his neck bulging.

Ouch, you shouldn't have said that, I thought, as I waited the nano-second for Justi's retort.

'Don't you "lady" me, and yes, I know it's a public holiday. I'm a teacher here in Slovenia.'

I stepped in to try and defuse the situation and salvage any hopes of finding a room.

'Look, we can see you're very busy, but we don't need much. We just need a budget room. We'll even take a single room, and out of town is fine. Do you have anything?'

His pulse rate seemed to drop a little, and he scribbled addresses for two possible places and recommended the first, adding that the second was 'not very good'. He shoved the piece of paper angrily towards me across the desktop, and without another word, turned his attention towards a couple in ski suits who had stood behind us and witnessed our exchanges. I imagined they wished they were in the other queue to see his more friendly colleague.

We drove a short distance out of town to find the first place on our list of two, which if he was correct about the second not being good, was actually only a list of one.

It was an ancient, wooden chalet-type hostel that looked like a stereotypical cartoon haunted house. We were shown upstairs to the room by a young man who told us that the building was due to be demolished in the spring. We had to concentrate on walking carefully because the old floorboards were alarmingly twisted and warped as we creaked our way along the dark corridors. The room turned out to be a dormitory, and when we asked if the other guests wouldn't mind Bryn, the young man said, 'Sorry, no dogs in this room.'

He offered us the use of a small wire kennel at the rear of the building, but at a forecast minus ten degrees, that wasn't an option.

With our hope of finding a room rapidly running out, we asked the young man if he knew anything about the second place on our list.

'Ah, *ja*, you will like; it is in centre of town,' he told us before drawing a map on the back of our scrap of paper.

Back in the car, we looked at the map and were surprised to see just how central to town option 'b' was. The small apartment block had a side door with a faded sign that read 'Rooms, *Zimmer*, *Sobe*'.

We rang the bell and waited. A short dark-haired lady answered, and when we asked about a room, she opened the door wider and invited us inside, saying '*Ja*, I have room.'

'We have a dog. Can we bring him in?' I asked.

She paused for a moment, maybe because her English was not too good, then to our relief she replied, '*Ja*, dog OK.'

She showed us to the room which, though very basic, was clean and warm. The bed and wardrobe looked to be nearing the end of their useful lifespan, and a threadbare rug lay on the linoleum floor. She then showed us along the corridor, which was lit with dim, incandescent bulbs without shades, to see the shared bathroom. Like our room, the bathroom looked like a blast from a 1970s past but was also perfectly adequate and clean.

'How much is it for the room?' we asked, hoping that the central location wouldn't mean a jacked-up price.

'Five thousand tolars per night,' she replied in a tired-sounding, take-it or leave-it way.

A quick calculation equated it to about £15 per night, which seemed exceedingly low, even by our budget standards, and we agreed to stay for five nights. It appears that 2003 may have been a time of change and new beginnings in Kranjska Gora, as by the following year, both of the guesthouses on our list had ceased to be. Over the next few years, more modern hotels, pensions and restaurants sprang up in and around the town, and no doubt the prices too.

While locating a car park nearer to our new-found accommodation, we realised it was only about 100 metres from the tourist office and surmised that our friend behind the desk had hoped we'd be staying in the old wooden hostel, as far away as possible.

It was a wonderful holiday. We enjoyed many hours on the fantastic cross-country ski tracks that followed the valley floor and led uninterrupted over the border into Italy. Bryn loped alongside us, his dark coat gleaming in the bright sunshine against the sparkling snow. Although he was now almost fourteen years old, he was invigorated by the new terrain with its fascinating new sights and smells; he seemed in his prime once more.

Unlike cross-country skiing, which is free, downhill skiing is an expensive game, but as we'd unexpectedly managed to save some pennies with our cheap accommodation, we decided to spend our last day on the piste. The snow conditions were excellent as we weaved our way down the slopes busy with people enjoying the clean rarefied alpine air, and with a picture-postcard backdrop of the magnificent snow-covered peaks of the Julian Alps.

That evening, as we lay tired but still exhilarated in our room, we happily recalled the best bits of our holiday. After a while, as our elation began to ebb, Justi became more thoughtful and serious.

'Can you see us going back to the UK after the school year ends in July?' she asked.

'Er, well, I'm not sure. I'd like to spend more time in this area, but it's not really possible, is it? I mean, we're a bit too far away in Podpetek to visit the Julian Alps regularly, even if we had more money.'

'Yes, that's true, but it's not just here. There are lots of places in Slovenia we haven't seen yet. I'm not ready to go home. Are you?'

'After this week, certainly not. I want to see these mountains in the summer too. Let's look into ways to stay a bit longer.'

With this conversation in mind, Justi began to make tentative enquiries when she returned to school. She discovered that the Ministry of Education would be continuing to fund the foreign language assistant scheme for the foreseeable future. She also learned that it might be possible to apply for a transfer to another school within Slovenia.

It was a risky strategy, though, as the options for the teachers concerning the type of school and the chosen locations were very limited. Only about 50 schools in the whole of Slovenia were involved in the scheme, and they weren't necessarily located near to the Julian Alps. It also meant that she wouldn't know until July if she was successful.

'I won't have enough time to apply and accept another teaching job if we're hanging around waiting to hear from the Slovene schools till July,' she said.

But it seemed that Slovenia was starting to get under our skin, and we both wanted to experience and learn more about this little green jewel of a country. By the end of the week, Justi had applied to stay in the school system but had requested a transfer to another school. She gave her preferred location on the form as 'NW Slovenia' and added 'near the mountains'.

Chapter 14 A Whirlwind Tour

As fast as the winter had arrived in Podpetek, so it left; the snow disappeared in a matter of days, and the air became warm, alive with the sound of busy insects commencing their springtime duties. The forests were filled with carpets of pale hellebores, while swathes of white spring crocuses spread across the fields. We were getting to like this well-defined transition of the seasons; it meant that we could make plans, knowing what weather to expect. It had been tough to do that in Scotland when our best chance of enjoying a couple of weeks of fine summer weather had meant booking a trip on the bike bus.

In Podpetek, as in most Slovene towns, it was a case of putting the skis away and getting the bikes out again. This seasonal change is noticeable in most of the big sports chains in Slovenia, when, within a matter of days, all the winter equipment is removed and the shops are filled with bikes, tennis rackets, rollerblades, camping equipment and beach paraphernalia.

I started riding my bike again and, within a few days, had formulated an 80-kilometre morning training ride that made a convenient loop through the spectacular green countryside. I would wake early to prepare our breakfasts, and when Justi had left for work, I'd take Bryn for an hour's walk in the coolest part of the morning before heading out on my bike. As my fitness increased, I'd complete my ride in just over two and a half hours and be back in plenty of time to do the daily chores before Justi arrived home again.

My route took me past beautiful old churches and roadside shrines painted with ancient frescoes. I contoured along hillsides where locals worked in the vineyards, tending to the vines and making repairs after the ravages of winter. Beekeeping is a great tradition in Slovenia, and I noticed rows of hives in many of the fields. The bright colours of the beehives stood out sharply against the rejuvenating light green of the spring grass, and many of them had artistic pictures, depictions of traditional folk tales, painted on their wooden panels.

Once a week, after returning from my ride, I'd mow the lawn for Bojana and Igor. On the first occasion, just as I was finishing the grass, Bojana leant over her balcony, wiggling a bottle in one hand and a glass in the other.

'Roy, come, have veeskey!'

It was only 10 a.m., and already, the sun was beating down. The prospect of drinking shots of whisky wasn't an appealing one. I joined Bojana and Igor on their shady, grapevine-covered balcony and politely asked if a glass of water or juice might be on offer instead. Bojana frowned and looked puzzled by my request.

'No veeskey? But you are Scottish, yes?'

'No, I'm not Scottish. I lived in Scotland, but I'm from Liverpool, England,' I tried to explain.

This had been a common theme since I'd arrived in Slovenia, and despite my broad Liverpudlian accent, many Slovenes on first meeting me think I'm Scottish. I've never managed to get to the bottom of that particular confusion, and even after many years in the country, it still happens.

With a dismissive shrug of the shoulders, Bojana obliged my Sassenach weakness with a cold glass of homemade apple juice, and I sat and chatted with them in our international 'Sloglish' language. These chats became a happy weekly interlude after finishing my gardening duties.

Like many older Slovenes, Bojana and Igor retain fond memories of their younger days when their country initially thrived under the leadership of President Josip Broz Tito. There was undoubtedly a dark side to the years of communist rule in old Yugoslavia, but on the whole, the regime was a comparatively benign one.

One day, Bojana proudly produced a black and white photo of a pretty young girl handing a bunch of flowers to a smiling President Tito.

'Me,' she said, tapping her chest firmly, 'here in Podpetek.'

She went on to tell me about her meeting with the most powerful man of the old Yugoslavia. With Igor helping to translate, Bojana chuckled as she told me the story of how a town official, who was meant to present Tito with the flowers, had suddenly collapsed and died from a heart attack brought on by sheer panic at the impending task. With Tito already approaching the presentation hall and only seconds to spare, the body of the poor official was whisked away into a side room, the flowers were thrust into Bojana's arms, and she was delegated to welcome the President instead.

Igor recounted the terrible tale of his childhood when his two older brothers discovered a strange metal item in a corner of their garden as they played. It was a grenade from WW2 and both his brothers died when it tragically exploded.

Our lovely hosts shared many stories and gave me fascinating glimpses of life in old Yugoslavia. I'll always remember these relaxed and friendly chats with great fondness, and humility too.

*****

As the May holiday week approached, Justi and I planned another trip to see more of Slovenia. This time, we wanted to visit the Slovenian coast to the south before driving north over a mountain pass to Kranjska Gora. The weather forecast was perfect, and when the day arrived, we packed the car with camping equipment, and I attached my bike to the roof rack. It was a refreshing change to be heading towards the coast. The countryside around Podpetek was undoubtedly stunning, but both of us had felt the first twinges of a need to experience a different landscape. The forested hills around our town had begun to seem a little monotonous, and the views from the local summits shared the similar vista of yet more steep-sided hills in every direction, usually capped with a small church or chapel.

Justi had also mentioned that she would like to see a fast-flowing stream or river again like the ones she'd loved in Scotland and Wales. Although Podpetek had a small river running through the town centre, it was very sluggish even in the spring and would likely become a mere trickle as the hot summer months approached. We made sure to include a visit to the little town of Kobarid to see the famous River Soča that flowed along the impressively alpine Trenta Valley.

The first part of our journey took us south through the old town of Brežice before we stopped for some lunch in Bela Krajina, an area famous for its white birch forests. We sat by the serene River Kolpa where we watched a heron stalking among the reeds and saw the unmistakable electric blue flash of a kingfisher against the dark water.

Turning west, we passed the vast, foreboding forests of Kočevje, home to Slovenia's population of brown bears, then on to see the famous intermittent lake at Cerknica. Rowing boats lay incongruously at the edges of flat meadows that would become the bottom of the colossal lake within 24 hours of the heavy autumn rains. The lake water rises and falls through a series of underground subterranean passages where fish could find a haven in times of drought.

We continued past Postojna, the home of an amazing cave system that has been one of Slovenia's most popular tourist attractions since the 1800s. Having visited the caves on my day trip in the 80s, I would have liked to relive the experience again with Justi, but our budget wouldn't allow it this time around.

We turned south again in the Great White Chariot, and just before evening, we found a campsite on a high prominence above the sea near a town called Izola. As we set the tent up in the fading light, the chirp of the crickets began to lessen, and we saw the silhouette of a flock of wading birds whizz by overhead.

'I need this,' said Justi as I handed her a plate of hastily made, watery-looking noodles.

'Well, I don't think it'll be very tasty. We haven't got any sauce and...'

'No! Not that. I mean the sea; I need the sea,' she went on.

I was only teasing her; I knew what she really meant. I was from a seaport, and we'd both lived in the west of Scotland, just a short distance inland. Justi had also lived on the North Wales coast, where she looked out onto the sea every day from her cottage. As we watched the sun setting over the wide expanse of the Adriatic Sea, we reflected on just how important a place the ocean was to us both after a few months of living in landlocked Podpetek.

The Slovenian coastline is less than 45 kilometres long, and we spent the next two days exploring some of its highlights, such as the beautiful medieval town of Piran and the old salt pans at Strunjan. It was tough to leave the coast after such a short visit, but we were very excited about seeing more of Slovenia. We headed inland again and drove north through the Vipava Valley, which is one of Slovenia's great wine areas. To the north, a steep wall of hills known simply as the *Gora* (mountains) rose from the valley floor. We made a mental note of their location, hoping to find out more for future investigation.

As we headed further north, the hills became higher, and a mountain called Krn came into view, which is the southernmost peak of the Julian Alps. We arrived at the little town of Kobarid, where Ernest Hemingway had been stationed as an ambulance driver in WW1. We'd read that the town had a renowned museum with thousands of artefacts that tell the story of those terrible times. After giving Bryn a walk, we left him dozing in the car and set out to find the museum. As Kobarid is such a small town, it only took us a moment to locate the small building where an old artillery gun and a huge shell case stood on the pavement either side of the door.

Only ever having heard about Britain's involvement and the awful battles on the Western Front, it was a shocking eye-opener to discover that over a million men had lost their lives here in a series of offensives that lasted more than two and half years. We learned that all the hills and mountains in the area have bunkers and gun emplacements on their ridges and summits. The amount of human energy and heartbreak poured into these mountains was unfathomable. We left the museum feeling shocked and saddened and went in search of our campsite and a bar.

The site was wonderfully peaceful and seemed to be used mainly by canoeists as it was on the banks of the amazing River Soča. It was just as the books and websites had described when we'd first looked into Slovenia as a holiday destination during that cold wet Highland winter; the water really was that bright emerald green colour.

In the late afternoon, we followed a track close to the river to see a beautiful waterfall hidden in a fairy-like grotto of steep, dark rocks. On the way, we passed numerous WW1 bunkers. The contrast between man's ugly constructions of war and the unbelievable natural beauty of the land was stark.

The next day, we continued north and stopped for a cuppa in the town of Bovec. Although we'd only been driving for about 25 minutes, we noticed how the town looked so different from Kobarid. Gone were the small red Mediterranean roof tiles and large pots of oleanders that graced Kobarid. The architecture in Bovec was more alpine, and the houses had window boxes that would soon be filled with geraniums. It was an upbeat, adrenalin-filled little town where extreme canoeists rubbed shoulders with canyoners and skydivers. The wide, flat floor of the valley allowed the town to have a small airfield, while the steep surrounding mountains were home to skiing and mountaineering.

A few kilometres north of Bovec, we turned right, following signs for the Vršič Pass that would lead us over the mountains to Kranjska Gora and some more familiar ground. As we drove along the valley, we exclaimed in awe at its majestic beauty; it certainly seemed comparable to the wonders of Lauterbrunnen. The bright turquoise colour of the Soča River appeared to increase in intensity the nearer we drove to its source until it became almost iridescent.

We camped at Lepena where the river narrows and runs rapidly through a dramatic rocky gorge. Although we'd managed to do some short walks on our trip, I was feeling the need for something a bit more energetic.

'Would you mind driving up the steep Vršič Pass alone tomorrow?' I asked Justi that evening. 'I'd like to cycle it if that's OK with you.'

'Sure,' she said. 'How long d'you think you'll need?'

'I'll leave a couple of hours before you, and we can meet at the summit.'

'Are you sure you feel fit enough? You'll probably feel wrecked even if you get to the top, but don't worry, I'll be your broom wagon and sweep you up if you can't manage it,' said Justi with an evil glint in her eye. 'Or I might just give you a regal wave as I cruise past you in the Chariot,' she added wickedly.

The next morning, I got up early, eager to get going before the sun could do its worst, grabbed a bowl of cereal and filled my water bottles. Opening the tent door a little, I whispered into the gloom, 'See you on the top of the pass.' This resulted in a low groaning sound coming from Justi's sleeping bag, which I translated roughly as 'Go away you annoying idiot!'

Bryn showed only a bit more interest by sitting up in the back of the Chariot, circling once, and then making himself comfortable again before I'd got my bike off the roof rack. I felt invigorated as I rode along the Trenta Valley in the fresh, clear air of the May alpine morning. I passed by fairy-tale, timber-built houses and a little church, all of them adorned with wooden shingle roofs. The mountains rose from the valley floor so steeply that they gave a feeling of entrapment, and it was difficult to imagine how, and where, the road would scale its way out.

Then, a short distance after passing through the hamlet of Trenta, the answer to that question came in the first of 26 numbered hairpin bends. I took a gulp of water and began the long, steady ascent of what was then Slovenia's highest tarmac road. For the first few kilometres, the going was steep and the bends tight, but the distances between them were relatively short. I managed to get into a good rhythm but felt a twinge of cramp in one of my calves. However, I was feeling the benefit of my Podpetek training rides and a long section between bends that had an easier gradient gave me a chance to recuperate. The twinges of cramp didn't develop any further.

Eventually, I could see the top of the pass with its mountain hut still some distance away, but I was now feeling sure that I'd get there—comfortably. As I stood up on the pedals to haul myself up the final hairpin bend, a coach lurched around the corner to begin its perilous descent. He wasn't taking any prisoners, and I had to pull quickly over to my right and ride in the gravel for a few metres as he swung around the bend, blaring his horn noisily. I cycled on to reach the summit pass sign and stood astride the crossbar on my bike. A hiker walking by congratulated me with a 'Bravo!' and I felt pleased with my ride. I'd made good time and didn't feel wrecked, as Justi had suggested I would. I cycled back the short distance to the mountain hut, bought myself a bottle of cold shandy beer and sat in the sunshine to take in the view.

The sound of a horn, which I recognised as being from the coach that had just passed me, drifted up from below. I imagined the driver sounded the horn on most bends, like we'd heard the post buses in Switzerland do on our cycling holidays, but this sounded more cacophonous and persistent. The horn blowing continued unabated for some minutes, and I thought I could hear the sound of an engine being revved wildly. I looked at my watch and thought, *Justi should've been here by now* as I sipped my ice-cold drink and took my shoes and socks off to wriggle my toes in the sheep-cropped alpine grass under a cloudless azure sky. Just as I was starting to drift off, I spotted the Great White Chariot winding its way up the pass. As Justi came around the final bend, I sat by the roadside and wiggled my hand at her in a regal wave.

She pulled over into a parking bay and switched the scorching engine off. She looked shaken and distraught.

'There was a coach, and I got stuck on a bend, and he kept inching forward. There were cars behind me, and I couldn't go back. He kept blaring his horn and…'

She was almost in tears as she related the stressful incident while the Chariot's engine clicked and clinked as it began to cool down. It must have been a horrible situation, and it wasn't till many weeks later that I'd dare make a joke about looking wrecked and regal waves.

After a cold beer, Justi started to feel better, and we began to descend the 24 bends on the other side of the pass that leads to Kranjska Gora. Although shorter, the road is even steeper on this side of the pass, and Justi tensed as we approached every bend, expecting to meet another belligerent bus driver. The views of the Julian Alps were spectacular, and we marvelled at the engineering of the road that had been constructed by Russian prisoners in harsh conditions during WW1.

Halfway down the pass, we passed the ornate Russian chapel that was built to commemorate the prisoners who had lost their lives in an avalanche. We stopped in Kranjska Gora for a short break and to see what the town looked like without snow. Like any ski town just after the winter season, it looked tired as it waited to be regenerated by the summer hikers and coach parties. It was still too early in the season for climbing the mountains of the Julian Alps; the high, waymarked routes lay under snow, and the huts were still closed. Because of this, we camped further down the valley near a village called Dovje and satisfied ourselves with walking on lower hills and trekking up the Vrata Valley that leads to the north side of Triglav.

With the wildflower meadows starting their first bloom and with the backdrop of jagged, snow-covered peaks, we decided we'd found a mountain paradise. At the time, we were using the only available English guidebook to the Julian Alps area, and while it had been a great help, it was becoming out of date. As we walked on smaller hills near the picture-postcard Lake Bled, we found that trees had obliterated some of the open views described in the book, and one or two of the paths had fallen into disuse.

A thought crept into Justi's head and settled into one of her brain's storage cupboards that something should be done to remedy the problem. It would be in July, during another visit to the area, when that particular thought would emerge again.

Having made a huge circular loop of Slovenia, we began to make our way back to Podpetek with one more planned stop in the medieval town of Škofja Loka. Jelka had told us about a friend of hers who would be happy to show us around. We met Ajda (pronounced *eye-dah*) in a car park just outside the old town centre on another warm and sunny spring day. Ajda is a lovely sounding name and quite common for a girl in Slovenia. It means buckwheat, which for many of us may sound an odd name to give your daughter. Ajda was an attractive young woman in her early 30s who had recently married and moved to her husband's village where they'd built a new house.

After sharing her time and knowledge during an enjoyable walk around the old town, she invited us for tea at her new house. As she poured the tea, Ajda told us that, despite being happily married, she felt she would never get used to living in such a different part of Slovenia than she came from.

'Oh, that's a shame, Ajda. Whereabouts in Slovenia are you from?' asked Justi.

'You see that church over there,' said Ajda, pointing at a spire through the window that looked to be no more than a kilometre away. 'That's where my village is.' Her voice trailed off sadly.

Justi and I shot each other a surprised glance.

'But, Ajda, it's only about a kilometre away. Surely it can't be that different here?' Justi asked, both surprised and curious.

'Well, it will always be my village, my place. It's different here, and the people are different,' Ajda explained.

She seemed mildly shocked when we told her how many times we'd moved for reasons of work and, mostly, adventure.

'But you still have a house and place that you will return to whenever you can?' she asked.

'Er, no, not exactly. We don't know where we'll be one year to the next. It depends on where we can find work in a landscape that inspires us,' we tried to explain.

Although she was interested, it was evident that Ajda didn't understand our motivation or life choices.

Over the years, we've found that Slovenes are great travellers—you'll find them anywhere on the planet—but they rarely like to move far from their beloved roots.

Chapter 15 The Red Town

The end of Justi's first school year in Slovenia was already within sight. It was now almost June, and even though we'd only been away from Podpetek for a week, it seemed that high summer had arrived in our absence. The fields had become lush meadows carpeted with a blaze of wildflowers, and the new green foliage of the beech forests was dense and shady. Justi and I cycled in the afternoons and would often stop at one of the roadside bars to enjoy a cold drink and take in the view. On one particular day, Justi put down her beer for a moment and commented, 'I've always thought it's usually the old men of a country that define the nature of the land and the local traditions.'

'How do you mean?'

'Well, imagine two old Frenchmen gesticulating through the smoke of their Gauloises, or an old Irishman playing the fiddle with a pint of Guinness in front of him. Stereotypes, of course, but still they immediately conjure up an image of their country. But in Slovenia, I think it's the older women that define it. Look at that bunch over there, for example.'

I turned to see a group of elderly ladies bent double in the fields, tending to the narrow strip of vegetables and flowers that each local family seemed to own. They'd arrived on rusty old bikes, wearing pinafore dresses printed with flowery paisley designs and their heads covered with scarves.

'They're as tough as old boots,' she remarked, as we set off cycling again.

About ten minutes later, we found out just how tough they were. I was a bit ahead of Justi, and as I rounded a bend on a steep section of road, a large noisy tractor overtook me. Two men sat in the high cab while an old lady stood on the triangle of iron that attached the trailer to the tractor. As the driver fumbled to change into a higher gear at the top of the rise, the tractor halted for a second then suddenly lurched onward again. I heard, rather than saw, the sickening thud as the old lady lost her hold and landed on the road. The massive wheel of the trailer rode over her legs, and the tractor carried on, the men oblivious to her plight. I leapt off my bike to try and assist her, but she was already starting to stand up. Blood trickled down her face from a cut above her eye, and her torn dress revealed a massive bruise and several cuts on her legs.

Justi had joined us, and we both tried to make the old lady stay put while we offered her some water. She was having none of it, though, and was more concerned about brushing the road dust off her clothes before limping on in a doggedly determined way along the road. We walked with her until the younger of the two men in the tractor came jogging back along the road, having noticed that granny was missing. We offered him a phone to get medical help, but the gesture was abruptly declined by both the old lady and him with a strong, '*Ne!*' The tractor stood with the engine running a little further along the road, and as the driver lowered the rear door, the young man helped the old lady into the back of the empty trailer. We watched as it chugged and rattled its way along the road until it turned down a lane and disappeared from view behind the tall hedges and trees. For a long time after, we often wondered about her and imagined that her wounds would have been treated with carefully prepared medicines she would likely have made herself.

It was the last week of school, and the atmosphere had lifted from one of exam stress to holiday jubilation. The kids put on a raucous play that seemed to be attended by most of the town. Justi was given a beautiful white-gold pendant as a leaving present from the school. We were also both humbled when we received gifts from our friends in the form of locally made glass crystal wine goblets, clocks and other mementoes.

During that last week, Justi also received a letter from the Ministry of Education. She opened it during breakfast, and her face broke into a smile as she eagerly read it.

'C'mon, what does it say?' I asked, impatient and excited.

'Well, my application was successful, and a school near the Julian Alps want an English teacher.'

'Wow, fantastic! Where's the school? Is there a problem?' I asked as Justi's initial enthusiasm seemed to wane a little, and a frown formed across her cheery face.

'That might be the only downside. The school's in Jesenice, that ugly town with the steel factory we passed on the motorway.'

'Oh,' I said, also feeling a little deflated, as we both remembered the grubby-looking industrial town we'd seen from the motorway. It had contrasted so sharply with its amazingly scenic alpine surroundings. 'Well, it mightn't be so bad. Let's go and have a look and see what the school and town are really like,' I suggested.

'Yes, I agree,' said Justi. 'I'll arrange a meeting with the headteacher of the school next week.'

When Justi told her colleagues in Podpetek that she would be going for an interview to teach in Jesenice, the response was a mixture of surprise and negative comments about the town.

'Jesenice! It's an awful place; we call it the red town because of all the iron dust from the steelworks,' commented Jelka, echoing the opinion of most of our friends.

Some even suggested that the children of Jesenice would be less well behaved than those of Podpetek.

The guys in the cycling club were equally dismissive about the town but agreed that the cycling in the area would be good, with plenty of steep mountain passes. While we mulled over the surprisingly hostile comments, we both believed, and hoped, that it might have been a slight over-reaction on their part. While we respected the opinions and advice of Justi's colleagues, who had always appeared clear thinking and informative, it seemed that their views of Jesenice might be skewed for reasons we weren't quite sure about.

'Remember how rooted the Slovenes are; remember Ajda,' said Justi. 'I imagine like most folk, they only pass Jesenice on the motorway and never actually go into the town.'

While we tried to convince ourselves with reason and logic that Jesenice wouldn't be as bad as friends and colleagues portrayed it, we still had niggling doubts. We needed to find out for ourselves.

The day after school broke up, we packed the Chariot with our camping equipment and headed to Jesenice. Justi had arranged a meeting with Polona, the headteacher of the primary school who had enrolled in the language assistant scheme. We planned to spend at least a week camping and walking in the mountains, or maybe a bit longer if our finances would allow.

This time, instead of bypassing Jesenice on the motorway, we turned off to drive through the town and see if it was as bad as everyone we knew suggested it was. We were pleasantly surprised. Although many thousands of tourists pass by it during the holiday seasons, it's not a tourist town, but nor does it claim to be. It's a town that's proud of its industrial heritage, based solely around iron and steel, but there was no sign of the red dust our friends had told us about. About midway through the town, we passed the railway station with its grey concrete, communist façade. Its appearance gives no hint that it's an important international border crossing where trains arrive from Croatia, Serbia and beyond before crossing into Austria, and vice versa.

The streets were litter-free, the shops busy, and like the railway station, the town looked functional. That's not to say that the inhabitants don't try to improve its looks; we noticed that window boxes of colourful geraniums adorned many of the high-rise apartments. We stopped at a newly built shopping centre to stock up for our trip just before we left the town. People sat outside the supermarket café bar under large sun umbrellas, enjoying a cold drink and a break from buying their groceries.

'Jesenice seems fine to me. What do you think?' I asked Justi as we headed out along the road towards Kranjska Gora in the scenic upper Sava Valley.

'Yes, it's OK, but I'm not sure I want to live there.'

If Justi were successful in her interview with Polona, then once again, the school would be obliged to find us a place to live, and although neither of us said it, we knew that the accommodation would most likely be in the town. We stopped once again at the campsite near the village of Dovje and pitched our tent so that we had a great view of the mountains from the unzipped door. That evening, as I browsed through our out-of-date and out-of-print guidebook to the Julian Alps, Justi shared the idea that she'd stowed away in the back of her mind on our previous trip.

'Maybe we should contact the publishers and ask if they would like their book updating. If we're seriously going to stay here for another year,' she went on, 'then we would be well placed to do it.'

'Really? Do you think so?' I asked, intrigued to hear more.

'Well, if I get this teaching job, we're going to be exploring a lot of these mountains this year, so it would make sense to at least note any changes made since the book was written. You could do some hills during the week, and then at weekends, we can walk some together.'

'What a great idea!' My heart and head were instantly filled with happy thoughts of spending long days in the mountains and indulging in my passion for landscape photography.

'Don't get too carried away. We'll have to email the publishers first, and I haven't got the job yet!'

Early the next morning, Justi had to drive back into town to meet Polona at the school. She dropped me off with Bryn at the head of the long Vrata Valley that leads towards Triglav, and we arranged to meet back at the camp around midday. I was keen to try and get some photographs of a well-known waterfall about halfway along, and it would give Bryn a good few hours' walk. I was earnestly hoping that Justi and Polona would decide they could work together and that the school was OK, but I wondered if we could accept the accommodation on offer if it meant living in the town.

I was also intrigued about the possibility of updating the guidebook; I believed it would help give me a deeper sense of purpose for my time spent in Slovenia. With this in mind, I scribbled in a notebook a description of my walk up the valley. The narrow path followed close by the crystal-clear river that sparkled in the shafts of sunlight falling through the tall fir and larch trees. The young river flowed from the foot of the north face of Triglav, and its pristine quality and beauty filled me with energy. I kept Bryn on his lead as I was now in the Triglav National Park, where signs by the track listed the dos and don'ts of park rules.

At the foot of the falls, a good number of day-trippers who had driven up the Vrata forest road stood looking up at the tumbling water and snapped pictures, while small groups of hikers passed each other on the narrow path that led directly up to the fall. I started up the steep path with Bryn, who was well used to such terrain, and despite his dog age being a ripe 98, he still seemed very game for an adventure. He'd never shown any sign of tiredness or displeasure during hundreds of wet UK hill days.

The sound of the falls soon grew louder, and as the path levelled, we rounded a bend to see the full might of the impressive cascade. We felt it too in the wet spray as rainbows and prisms of light bounced off the huge torrent of water that struck the rocks below in a boiling white cauldron.

A sizeable group of people hung around the rocks, waiting for their turn to snap a photo at the best viewing spots. They shouted and laughed excitedly as everyone tried to make their voices heard over the roar of the water. It was an incredible sight, but I wanted to get a photo that would be a little different from the hundreds taken every day. I also wanted to get away from the crowds.

I looked back across to the other side of the valley and noticed a break in the trees that should give a good view of the falls. I was determined to get a decent photo and even dared to think that it might end up in a published guidebook.

'C'mon, Bryn. Let's go, fella,' I called, trying to gauge Bryn's appetite for an extended walk which I expected might involve a lot of effort.

I was right; it did involve a lot of effort. Having made my way back down to the road, I backtracked to cross the river by a footbridge then started a diagonal ascent up the forested hillside on the opposite side of the valley. When I reached the break in the trees, I discovered that it was a steep, eroded gully. Bryn's enthusiasm appeared to have deserted him, and he was starting to look worried in that way that he had. I couldn't blame him; it was hot, and the terrain had become dangerously unpleasant. I tied his lead to a tree on the edge of the loose stony gully, and he lay down, happy to be excused from my strange obsession of staring into a black box.

I ventured out into the middle of the gully, slipping and trying to gain some balance as I took my rucksack off and set up my camera tripod. As I tripped the shutter on my ancient bellows film camera, my phone rang. I fumbled in my rucksack and almost sent my camera down the gully but managed to grab the tripod as it started to topple over in nightmare slow motion. It was Justi.

'Hi, can you come into town in about an hour? There's an apartment Polona wants us t—'

The phone went dead as the signal was lost. I made sure my camera was safe and then teetered across the gully and climbed a little higher through the trees. Eventually, the phone gained a few nobbles of signal strength. I called Justi back.

'Polona has an apartment to show us, but it's in town. Can you get here on the bus in about an hour?'

Justi sounded excited; her interview had obviously gone well.

'No, I'm sorry, there's no way I can get back for at least a couple of hours.'

'Oh, OK. I'll se—'

The phone went dead again. I felt I'd got my picture, so I packed my camera away in my rucksack and made my way back to Bryn who looked even more worried as I approached, my boots scattering a cascade of loose gravel down the gully. We made a rapid descent back down to the river and walked along the valley path and up to the campsite. A couple of hours later, Justi arrived and told me about her morning. The interview had gone well, and the school looked decent. Justi had also liked Polona, and she felt that they would get on well.

'Great, but what about the apartment?' I asked, curious to know if she'd come around to the possibility of living in Jesenice.

'Polona took me to see a flat that the school had found for us, but I wouldn't want to live there, so I said so,' she told me. 'It was in one of the high-rise apartment blocks in the centre of town—clean and bright and handy for work, but it's just not for us, or Bryn,' she said.

Having lived in idyllic rural cottages for the last fifteen or so years, I completely understood her reluctance to try and live in a noisy urban environment, even if it wasn't exactly a city.

'What are we going to do then?' I asked.

'I'm not sure. Polona told me she has a cousin who might be willing to rent a first-floor apartment in his house. He lives in a small village just outside Kranjska Gora, and we can go and see it tomorrow.'

'Sounds fantastic,' I said, but there was a hesitation in Justi's voice.

'I don't think we can take it. There's no phone line, and that means no internet.'

'Oh, I see,' I said sadly, knowing that the internet was vital so that we could keep in touch with family and friends and follow the news.

'It would also involve a 50-kilometre round trip every day,' Justi added.

Although that may not be a great distance to a lot of folk, we were trying to keep commuting to a minimum. The less time spent in a car, the better, we both thought. The school in Podpetek had been within walking distance of our apartment. The next morning, Polona arrived at the campsite in her car, and we followed behind her in the Chariot up the stunning upper Sava Valley. Polona had arranged with her cousin to show us the apartment, and despite our misgivings about the absence of an internet connection, we felt obliged to at least view it.

'It's a shame we won't be able to take the apartment. It's so beautiful here,' Justi lamented as we passed idyllic pastures with rugged mountains rearing up on either side.

Polona indicated, and we left the main road and followed her up a pass that was signed to Austria. After a short distance up this steep road, she turned into the drive of a house which had the typical overhanging eaves of an alpine chalet and a fine balcony on the first floor.

Janez and his wife, Ana, were sitting outside on their patio, enjoying the sunshine. They came to greet us, and we shook hands as Polona introduced us. Janez and Ana were an attractive couple in their early 60s, and they both looked fit and athletic. They also spoke fluent English, and we were very soon being asked why we'd chosen to come and live in Slovenia. Many Slovenes had asked us this question, but it didn't need a lengthy answer or explanation on that particular day. I smiled and swept my arm towards the magnificent view of flower meadows and rocky alpine peaks.

'This is why we came,' I said, knowing that Justi would have answered the same. Janez and Ana smiled; they understood. Ana and Polona went inside to make coffee while we followed Janez up an external flight of wooden stairs to see the apartment. The main room had a combined kitchen and dining area and was small though nicely decorated and finished with warm amber-coloured pine furniture and panelling. Janez opened a door, and we stepped out onto the covered balcony. The view was magnificent; wildflower meadows stretched into the distance, and the Julian Alps soared into the sky above the town of Kranjska Gora. The balcony was huge, with a sofa at one end and dining table and chairs at the other.

'We could use it as another room in the warmer seasons,' Justi commented.

'And we'd be able to store our bikes on it during the winter,' I mused.

Justi went right to the nub of the matter and turned to Janez. 'Janez, we like the apartment very much, but there are two things we're bothered about. First of all, it's a long way from the school. All that driving will make it expensive.'

'But you'll get travel expenses.'

'What? Because I choose to live up here rather than within walking distance of school?'

'In Slovenia, public service staff get travel expenses from their home to their work. One of the benefits left over from communism,' Janez said with a smile.

'Wow, I didn't realise that. But the other thing is, I believe there isn't a phone line, so no internet. Is that right?'

'Hmm, there's not a phone line, but we do have cable to the house. It will be possible to get a wireless router, and you can get the internet that way.'

We both looked at him blankly.

'What's a router?' Justi asked. It was still early days with regard to internet technology.

'Let's go and have some coffee, and I'll explain.'

Over coffee, Janez explained this strange new option and even offered to pay for it. It was a done deal as we'd already fallen in love with the little apartment in its idyllic location. Polona excused herself and left for work while we spent a happy hour or so chatting with our new landlords. We learned that Janez had been an Olympic skier, racing for Yugoslavia in the 1970s. They'd built the house as their weekend retreat and lived about an hour away in a town further to the east.

Ana showed Justi a part of the garden that we could use to grow vegetables, and she confirmed that Bryn would be welcome in the apartment. It was all we needed to know, and I pictured Bryn warming his old bones on the sunny balcony. Once again, we were delighted to have found a lovely apartment; the rent was very reasonable, and the landlords were friendly and fair. Janez handed over a set of keys to the apartment and told us to move in whenever it suited us.

It felt like the start of an exciting new stage in our lives. We had finally arrived on the Sunny Side of the Alps.

Chapter 16 Triglav

Feeling elated by the prospect of living so close to Slovenia's Julian Alps, we made a few sorties into the mountains. To test our fitness, we first climbed Stol, the highest mountain of the Karavanke range. The Slovene side of the Karavanke Mountains is generally more forgiving than the vertical world of the Julian Alps. Nevertheless, the grassy forested slopes are steep and long, so it was with relief that we finally reached the airy summit rocks. The Austrian side plunged steeply into a green valley where we could see groups of hikers leaving a mountain hut to make their way up via a path that clung to the sides of a wild corrie.

Despite being concerned that the ascent might have been a hill too far for Bryn, he'd shown that he was still very willing. He sat on the summit rocks with the breeze gently ruffling his soft black coat and sniffed the air as alpine choughs shrieked for attention, circling in the hope of sharing our sandwiches.

More glorious mountain days followed. We would start early, always careful to be back down in the valley before the late afternoon when storm clouds would gather in the humid air. The thunderstorms could be extreme, and the barrage of sound was exaggerated as it echoed off the hills and around the confines of the valley. If the storms didn't arrive, then we'd enjoy interludes of swimming. We bathed our tired bodies in the warm water of Lake Bled with its fairy-tale church sitting atop its little island. The backdrop of the castle on its lofty, craggy perch, with Stol dominant on the skyline, made a perfect chocolate-box photo image.

Towards the end of the week, we discussed the need to get back to Podpetek to begin the process of moving. We had to inform Bojana and Igor of our plans as well as the various Slovene authorities. We still had the school holiday time ahead of us, so we also wanted to check the possibility of finding a cheap flight to the UK. We could combine seeing family with a trip up to the Highlands to retrieve some of our belongings from our friends' lofts and garages.

However, I was unwilling to leave without attempting to climb Triglav. I felt fit and eager and wanted to round our excellent week off with a big day. Justi was happy to have a rest day so she could catch up with emails at an internet café. She also wanted to send an email off to the guidebook company to suggest that we could update their book. Bryn looked more than happy to have a rest day too, so with my rucksack packed, Justi drove me up the Vrata Valley early the next morning and dropped me off at the car park at the end of the road. With final deliberations and estimates of expected times for my return the following day, we hugged, and Justi got back into the Chariot with Bryn. I watched until they disappeared out of sight down the dusty gravel road.

I made my way past an attractive mountain hut and reached the turn-off for my chosen route up the mountain. A memorial to the partisans who fought in the Julian Alps during WW2 stood near the start of the path, a huge metal karabiner and piton that looked surreal in the early morning light. I headed off between the trees on the narrow waymarked path which immediately rose steeply through the dew-covered undergrowth. Pausing for breath, I watched a tiny black alpine salamander crawling between the gnarled tree roots. It was hot and sunny, and I was grateful for the shady forested start to my day.

Eventually, I reached the tree-line, and incredible views began to open out towards the stupendous 1,000-metre-high north wall of Triglav. The mountains on the opposite side of the valley also came into view, and I'm not ashamed to say that the beauty of the vista brought tears of joy and wonder to my eyes.

I put on my climbing helmet and harness at the foot of a steep section of rock and followed the waymarks as the route became more exposed to the vertical drops edging the path. Every so often, I stopped to take pictures and scribble notes, hoping they might be useful should we ever get the chance to work on a guidebook. It wasn't an ideal way to make a record as sometimes the pen wouldn't work, and the little notes started to disintegrate in my sweating hands.

I heard voices ahead of me on a particularly steep section and, looking up, I was surprised to see three adults and two young children. The kids were aged about seven or eight, and I watched impressed as they competently clipped their karabiners into the pegs and rungs of the near-vertical rock. As I passed them, we all exchanged a '*Dober dan*!' and I saw that it was a mother and father with their young son and daughter and presumably granddad. Mum and dad led the party, and it was obvious that they were all enjoying the sensational exposure and the feeling of the dry rock under their hands as they climbed. Granddad kept an experienced watchful eye on the kids' safety as he brought up the rear.

Slovenes are very adept in the mountains, and they learn their skills from a very young age. Although I was initially surprised to see such young children in an exposed situation on a big mountain, I've seen it many more times since. It used to be said that to qualify as a 'true' Slovene, citizens must climb Triglav at least once in their lives. Although Slovenes may have become more relaxed and less insistent about this sentiment, it still holds sway with many.

Eventually, the angle eased as I reached a vast barren lunar landscape of rocks that had to be crossed to reach the big Triglav mountain hut, which can sleep 200 people. I'd read that this was the *dom* where most Triglav aspirants stayed the night before making their way to the summit the following morning. Not far from the hut stands a massive buttress that gives access to the narrow ridge leading to the summit of Slovenia's highest mountain.

Hoping to avoid the noisy crowds of the large *dom*, I decided to head to a smaller mountain hut I'd spotted on my map. It would only add an hour or so to my next day's effort on Triglav, but I imagined I'd have a more peaceful night. I traversed the edge of the lunarscape on a waymarked path that led me to my chosen hut, which stood on a rocky plinth. The little building looked welcoming, its paned windows and shutters like cheerful, friendly eyes. I'd made good time; it was only just after lunchtime, and I could have pushed on to the summit as no storms were forecast. I wanted to savour the experience, though, so I ordered a bowl of soup in the hut and booked in for the night.

'It seems pretty quiet. Are there many people staying tonight?' I asked the hut warden.

'There are only three or four booked in at the moment, but that could change,' said the young man, a student from Ljubljana who had chosen to spend his summer working at the hut. He would only make a modest wage, but it was the experience of living high in the mountains that had attracted him to the job, he confided with enthusiasm. Knowing how hard the work can be, I hoped his enthusiasm would keep him going through the busiest part of the season.

I spent the afternoon exploring the area around the hut and sorting out my notes which described the route so far. I sat sipping a beer while admiring the stupendous view and watched the tiny figures of people descending from the surrounding steep summits. After enjoying a tasty bowl of goulash at about 8:45 in the evening, I thought about retiring to bed. I went outside to enjoy a last look at the views and watched as the sun bathed the tops of the peaks in a warm orange glow. It was an idyllic, peaceful setting, and I looked forward to a good sleep and doing it all again the following day.

I climbed the wooden stairs that led to the attic dormitory room and chose a place between the rows of neatly folded, heavy wool blankets. There did, indeed, only seem to be three other people staying, so a bit of comfort and space wasn't going to be an issue. Or so I thought. Just as I was starting to doze off, I was jolted awake by the sound of voices and laughter approaching the hut. The noises got louder and were soon accompanied by the noisy stomping of boots, followed by the unmistakable KER-CHACK! of the door latch being lifted. A boisterous clamour suddenly filled the hut as a large group of Slovenes piled in from the chilly evening air. I could hear drinks orders being shouted over the babble of voices.

'*Pivo*! (Beer!) Schnapps! Jägermeister!'

In another few moments, I heard an accordion accompanied by a guitar strike up a tune.

Damn, I thought, *so much for a peaceful night.*

However, as I lay wide awake but snug under the wool blankets, the cacophony of noise became transformed into melodic songs. Like the Highlanders, the Slovenes love their music, and they're good at it. I began to enjoy the tuneful singing and even started to drift off again, but my peaceful repose wasn't to last. In another two hours or so, with the singing finished, people burst into the dormitory to find themselves a bed for the night. Drunken, giggling partygoers packed in either side of me until the attic resembled a human can of sardines. The giggling, snoring, farting and laughter went on well into the night, but I knew it was all part and parcel of hut life.

The next morning, I was up and out before the revellers stirred, after a breakfast of bread, jam and fresh coffee. I made my way across rocky limestone slabs, criss-crossed with deep fissures, grykes and sinkholes. This type of terrain is known worldwide by the Slovene word *karst*. At first sight, this landscape looks dry, lifeless and forbidding, but even here, nature is full of surprises. Delicate, pale flowers like white poppies and purple bellflowers burst from tiny crevices in the sun-bleached rock.

The route steepened as it wound its way up a band of rock before reaching the level plateau where the big *dom* stands. This is the highest hut in Slovenia, and I was surprised to see a couple of sheep outside the building looking for alpine flowers to nibble amid the stony ground.

Sitting outside at a table, I scribbled more notes while watching groups of people like a column of ants make their way up the vertiginous buttress that led to the summit ridge. I finished my coffee and headed across the stony slopes towards the buttress, stopping on my way to chat to a group of Czechs returning from the summit. They were all tired but elated, huge grins lighting up their faces as they described how they'd driven from their home country only the day before to climb Triglav. They'd walked up to the hut in the evening and had arrived just before midnight. They were expecting to be down in the valley by midday and then to drive back to the Czech Republic after lunch. They hoped to get home to their beds at about one or two o'clock the following morning.

I was impressed by their dedication and energy, but I was also content to be enjoying all the sensations of the mountains at a somewhat slower pace. As I neared the foot of the buttress, I noticed a large patch of ice, about half the size of a football field, below the vertical crags. This was all that remained of the Triglav glacier that, not many years ago, had been much larger. Janez had told me how, in the 1970s, he used to walk up with his skis in the summer months and train on the glacier to keep his Olympic fitness and techniques sharp. Judging by the smooth, polished rock on the buttress, it was evident that Triglav was the most climbed mountain in the Julian Alps. A plethora of metal pegs, rungs and steel cables laced the rock, so although very exposed, the route has been made relatively safe. Because of this, Triglav is regularly climbed by folk who wouldn't usually attempt such an endeavour.

At the top of the buttress, I clipped into a cable on a steep section to let a middle-aged Slovene couple pass by on their descent. I was stunned to see they were carrying plastic shopping bags and wearing training shoes. Their casual clothes completed the image, as though they'd gone out to the shops and had somehow been mysteriously transported to the top of Slovenia's highest mountain. They didn't quite fit the bill compared to the lean and competent Slovene mountaineers that we'd met in the hills since we arrived here.

'*Dober dan*!' they said enthusiastically as they manoeuvred awkwardly past me, and I caught the strong smell of alcohol on their breaths as they passed. The lady's carrier bag dragged against the rock as she inched her hands along the steel cable, and I heard the unmistakable clink of a glass bottle. I suspected it was probably a bottle of schnapps taken up for a summit celebration.

I watched as they continued down the steep rocks, and despite their demeanour, they appeared to make good progress. Most Slovene people we've met have a very close affinity to their landscape, whether it's working on their vegetable plots, swimming outdoors or climbing their beloved mountains. I continued easily along the long narrow ridge, with huge drops on either side, to reach the final steep rocks and soon found myself on the summit of mighty Triglav—its name derived from an ancient three-headed deity.

The world was laid out below my feet, and an unending vista of mountains unfolded in every direction. It was an alpine paradise, and I daydreamt about the adventures that might lie in store for us during our next year in Slovenia.

A small metal shelter stands on the summit of Triglav, and I watched a group of Slovenes milling around it, laughing. One of them, bracing himself against the door, bent over while a friend beat him lightly on the backside with a piece of cord. So the story was true—it was obviously their first time on Triglav. It was mine too, but being a shy Brit, I decided not to request my inaugural spanking from the Slovenes and began the long descent to the valley to meet Justi.

I've seen a few odd things on the British hills over the years—people in fancy dress, a guy wearing nothing but his rucksack, and people popping bottles of champagne, to name just a few. But the Slovenes seem to have it beat, literally.

Chapter 17 Stormy Weather

Back in Podpetek, we booked a flight to the UK for the following week. It was still the era of cheap summer flights, and we were pleased with the price. We also told Bojana and Igor that we'd be moving to Jesenice by the end of August and had enjoyed staying in their apartment. They seemed genuinely sorry that we'd be leaving; I suspected that Bojana had missed having someone to look after once her daughter had left.

'Do you know of any local kennels that we could book Bryn into while we're in the UK?' I asked.

Bojana looked shocked. '*Ne*, Breen not stay in dog hotel. Breen stay here with us,' she said firmly. There was no arguing. 'Igor will walk Breen every day,' she informed us. Igor opened his mouth to say something but, with a resigned look, decided not to and just nodded in agreement.

We knew Bryn would be delighted with these arrangements; there was no doubt he'd be dining on fine food prepared by his doting personal chefs. The day before we were due to leave, we received a reply from the guidebook publisher. The director, Jonathan, had read our email with interest. He was unable to trace the whereabouts of the original guidebook writer and suggested that, rather than update the old book, we should write a new one. His proviso was that we should meet him before we started.

'Wow, that's brilliant!' I enthused to Justi, who was equally excited at the prospect. 'I imagine he wants to meet us to gauge how serious and committed we are to take it on. I wonder what he'll ask us?'

'His company has an office in the Lake District. We can call in on our way to or from Scotland when we go to see our friends.'

We left the warm weather and clear blue skies behind and flew into the UK under a leaden grey sky and summer drizzle. Cath and

Vic picked us up at the airport, and we were both bowled over when Cath told us she'd arranged extra insurance for her car so that we could use it for the week. This was very welcome news as Cath's car was a high-roofed people carrier and would be perfect for bringing some of our belongings down from Scotland. Cath and Vic had also generously offered us more loft and garage space in their house where we could store boxes until we needed them.

Although we were happy and excited about the new prospects, it seemed that our lives, as well as our belongings, were in a sort of suspended limbo. We couldn't see any further than a maximum of one year ahead. After a few days in Liverpool and Southport with family and friends, we headed north, having arranged that we would call in to see Jonathan at his office on our way back. It was lovely to see the Highlands again, but we only had time for one or two short walks in the glens in between returning loft space to our friends by filling Cath's car with boxes of our paraphernalia.

On the way back south, as we neared the small Lakeland town where Jonathan had his office, we again wondered what he would ask us.

'Maybe he wants to find out how well we know the Slovene mountains?' Justi speculated.

'Well, we don't yet. There's a whole lot more to the Julian Alps than Triglav,' I replied, feeling a little anxious as we pulled into the village car park.

'I think it was Richard Branson who once said, "If someone offers you an amazing opportunity, but you aren't sure that you can do it, say yes and learn how to do it later",' Justi said, sensing my nervous apprehension.

'Well, here we are.' I opened a door that displayed the publishing company's name on a smart brass plate. A friendly, smiling lady stood up from her desk and came over to greet us.

'Hi, we have an appointment to see Jonathan.'

'Oh right, you must be Justi and Roy from Slovenia. Please, follow me.'

We followed her up a flight of stairs and waited while she rapped on his office door and entered, briefly telling Jonathan we'd arrived.

'Come in, come in,' said a booming voice from somewhere inside, and we were waved in by his smiling assistant.

Jonathan stood up from behind his desk to shake our hands and proffer us seats. He seemed a larger-than-life character, full of energy and confidence gained from many years of experience and passion in his work. After a friendly chat, with Jonathan asking us how we'd come to be living in Slovenia, he coughed, sat up purposefully in his chair, stared intently at us in interview mode and asked, 'Have you written any books or articles before?'

A wave of nervous panic engulfed me, and I glanced at Justi, who, having attended professional job interviews before, was looking far more at ease. She calmly explained how, although she hadn't had the opportunity to write about general mountaineering topics, she had experience in writing articles in several academic journals and contributing to published reports, including one that involved an expedition to Iceland.

While Justi had Jonathan nodding appreciatively, I remembered two friends from Liverpool who had gone out to the US in the 1980s to forge a life in the star-studded Beverly Hills neighbourhood. One just missed gaining employment as Rod Stewart's gardener when the final stage of the interview involved questions about specific plant species; considering he'd only had experience in mowing his mum's lawn, he was obviously pretty good at winging it. His friend fared better and was taken on as Sylvester Stallone's chef despite his culinary skills amounting to producing nothing more haute cuisine than a Pot Noodle. He kept his boss happy (and in the dark) by ordering take-outs and having them delivered clandestinely to the back door of the kitchen.

It was my turn to answer, and Jonathan stared expectantly at me.

'Er, well, I wrote a short article about walking and climbing in the Swiss Alps for the British Diabetic Association, about, er,' I coughed, 'twenty years ago.'

'I see,' he said, looking and sounding justifiably unimpressed. 'Hmm, well… Do you know where this is?' he continued, turning in his chair to point at a large framed photograph on the wall behind his desk.

I looked up at the picture that depicted a rock climber in an athletic pose spread-eagled on an exposed crag with a backdrop of snow-covered pinnacles. In my head, someone shouted, 'Seize the day!' and despite being uncertain, I found myself answering with a confidence that surprised even me.

'That looks like Chamonix granite. Not sure of the route exactly, but it's a great photo.'

Jonathan's eyes lit up, and his face beamed. 'Yes, that's right. And that's my son climbing,' he added with unabashed parental pride.

That was the moment when we passed the test. Any residue of tension that remained disappeared when his smiling assistant came in carrying a tray of tea and biscuits. In a relaxed atmosphere, we chatted more, and we learned that, although his job demanded a lot of office hours, Jonathan got out in the hills whenever he could. He was passionate about mountains, and we eagerly shared what we'd already learned about the Julian Alps and the landscape of Slovenia.

'Well, I think that you should do some more walks, write them up and send them to us. If everything is OK, then we'll send you a copy of our contract to sign,' he said.

We left in agreement and made our way back to the car with smiles on our faces, feeling very pleased with our new project that involved climbing mountains.

Back in Slovenia, we busied ourselves with the chores of moving. We started packing boxes and bags and looked on as the enormous pile of diverse goods continued to grow alarmingly on our living room floor. In less than a year, we'd accumulated more stuff than we could now fit into the Chariot for a single journey to our new home. We'd had to buy bedding and kitchen items for our first apartment, and along with other items such as clothing and presents, it was clear that we would have to make two long trips across the country.

As we were mulling this inconvenience over, there was a knock on the door.

'Hey, how're you guys doing?' It was Jake and Mateja. 'We were wondering if we could come over to Kranjska Gora with you next week and see your new place? We'd like to do a bit of hiking in the mountains if there's enough time,' Jake went on.

Justi and I exchanged a knowing look.

'Yes, that would be lovely. Er, would you mind taking a few boxes in your car for us?'

'Sure, no problemo, buddy,' came Jake's enthusiastic reply.

However, his keenness seemed to wane a little as he and Mateja looked at our burgeoning mountain of goods.

'Don't be alarmed; most of that will go in the Chariot. There'll just be a few extra odds and sods,' I said, trying to reassure them.

'Odds and sods?' asked Jake with a puzzled look on his face.

I pointed to a few small boxes and bags while Justi explained another colloquial English-American anomaly.

Our day of departure arrived, and we said our goodbyes to Bojana and Igor. We were sorry to leave but also excited about the future. Bryn looked sorry too, as well he might, but Bojana gave him a cooked pork chop to make things easier for him.

Jake and Mateja had collected our boxes the evening before and had left early in the morning. They intended to go hiking near Kranjska Gora before meeting up at our new apartment. I was to drop Justi off in Ljubljana on the way at a television studio in the city centre. She'd been asked to make a voice recording for a CD to go with a new English coursebook to be used in the state schools. She planned to get the bus to Kranjska Gora as soon as she finished her work.

The first half of the journey was uneventful, but as we turned off for Ljubljana, we saw that the sky to the west had turned a menacing, inky black. Large drops of rain began bouncing off the windscreen as lightning strikes lit the clouds and distant mountains with an eerie, phosphorescent glow.

'I wonder how Jake and Mateja are getting on. I don't think they'll enjoy walking in that,' Justi said as I dropped her outside the recording studio.

As I approached the motorway turn-off for Kranjska Gora, the rain became torrential. Even with the windscreen wipers on overdrive, it was difficult to see the road ahead. Two police cars and a fire engine sped past with sirens wailing, their flashing lights adding vivid colour to the watery gloom. The road became noisy as the Chariot rattled over small stones that had been washed onto the surface from the verges. Squinting ahead, I could see that the police and a fire engine had come to a standstill. As I slowed, I saw that my lane was blocked by a deep bank of gravel that had flowed onto the road from the steep embankments. The fire crew dashed about, busily arranging temporary barriers while a policeman directed me onto the opposite lane, and I continued slowly. A hundred metres further on, another torrent of deep gravel and large rocks almost blocked the road, but I carefully inched past, knowing that soon the valley would become wider and the steep roadside embankments relent.

By the time I reached Kranjska Gora, it was clear that north-west Slovenia was experiencing an extreme amount of rainfall. More emergency vehicles scooted along the road with sirens screaming as they escorted dumper trucks and a lorry bearing a bulldozer en route to clear landslides of gravel and rocks.

I phoned Jake and Mateja to discover they were happily holed up in a café having only managed a short walk before the heavens opened. I found them sipping their third cup of coffee, and they told me how surprised they were to see me. They'd just heard from the bar staff that the road was now completely blocked by landslides.

I wondered if Justi would get through as it was the only road and bus route through to Kranjska Gora from Ljubljana.

'Come on, guys, I think we'll get up to our apartment OK, and you're welcome to stay. Even if the road opens, it would mean you wouldn't get back to Podpetek until the early hours.'

I drove up the pass with Jake and Mateja following and turned off the road. The house was dark, and Janez and Ana's car wasn't in the driveway. They'd probably seen the forecast and wisely stayed at home. Unloading a few essential items such as bedding, tea, bread and marmalade, we went up the stairs to the apartment and switched the lights on. The living room was bright and homely, and we soon began to relax and unwind. A deafening clap of thunder exploded above the house, abruptly cutting short this feeling of serenity and making the crockery rattle in the cupboards.

A few hours later, Justi phoned to tell me that she was on the bus and nearing Kranjska Gora. Thankfully, the emergency services had been working flat out and had managed to keep the road open, at least for the time being. The local roads resembled fast-flowing streams, so I left the Chariot parked in the drive and walked down with a large umbrella to meet her at the bus stop.

'What kind of a place have we come to?' Justi asked as we walked up the road, trying to avoid the deepest rivulets of muddy water. 'I hope this isn't normal summer rain,' she added.

Back in the apartment, Justi recounted her bus journey which had involved several stops as workmen desperately tried to clear sections of road inundated with storm debris. As she was talking, a deep rumble of thunder had the cupboard contents rattling again, and a pen, Justi's favourite, rolled from a worktop and dropped behind the fridge. Justi and Jake wriggled the fridge forward to recover it. She leaned behind the fridge to unplug it to gain a bit of extra space. As she unplugged it, the apartment suddenly went pitch black.

'Damn, it must have blown a fuse,' Justi said.

At the exact moment she'd unplugged the fridge, I'd been looking out of the window and seen that all the street lights and village houses had also been cast into darkness.

'I think it may be more than a blown fuse,' I said. 'Look outside.'

'Hey, did we do that?' cried Jake.

'Oh, heavens, surely we couldn't have done that,' whimpered Justi in horror.

The timing had been bizarre, but fortunately, it was nothing more than an extraordinary coincidence. It was another hour before power returned to the village, and during that time, I tried to reassure them that it wasn't their fault. Justi and Jake weren't to be persuaded, and they spent the time wracked with worry and guilt.

It had certainly been quite an introduction to our new life in the Julian Alps. That night, as we lay in bed listening to the dashing rain and rolls of thunder, we wondered what other challenges lay in store.

By the following morning, the storm had relented, but evidence of its ferocity was all around. Teams of workmen continued to clear roads of the torrents of rock and gravel that had been washed down the mountainsides. Electricity and communications engineers repaired fallen pylons and cables while police and fire crews continued to zip up and down the valley with sirens wailing and lights ablaze. We learned that the road had become impassable shortly after Justi's bus had got through and had only reopened at 10 a.m.

By lunchtime, the sky had cleared, and the sun came out. The four of us enjoyed a short walk before we waved Jake and Mateja off. We hoped that the next time they came, the weather would be a bit kinder.

Chapter 18 The Demise of the Great White Chariot

It was now mid-August, but there was still time before Justi began teaching in her new school for us to make a start on the walks for the guidebook. We bought two hand-held tape recorders to track all our routes as I'd already found that scribbling notes wasn't very practical. I was also excited about indulging in my passion for landscape photography for the guidebook. The cost of shooting lots of rolls of film concerned me, as we were still living on a tight budget. So I was delighted to find a camera shop just over the border in Austria that would develop a roll of slide film for only one euro, and I bought enough film to keep me going for a few months through a low-cost mail-order company.

For the rest of the summer, we gathered local information, bought maps and spent long days walking in the Julian Alps. We used our old, out-of-date guidebook as a starting point for many of our chosen hills and routes. We also added new mountain walks and different locations. Sometimes, we'd spend a day or two on a particular hill or path, recording the route meticulously and taking many photographs, only to realise that it wouldn't be suitable for inclusion in the book. This might be because the route was little used and badly waymarked or simply because there was no reliable public transport or any decent accommodation at the start or finish.

Often we walked together, but on several occasions, we walked alone to complete as many routes as possible before the start of the school term. Justi would then need the Chariot to get to work, which would make things more difficult for me to get to the beginning of some of the walks I'd do in the autumn.

In the evenings, after returning from our walks, we'd listen to our tapes, and each of us would tap out a transcript on the computer. Later, Justi would polish and fashion the transcripts (OK, correct my poor grammar) and turn them into a readable description of the walks. More than once, tempers flared as we argued over subtle word differences and descriptive text.

'It's just a small crag, not an outcrop.'

'No, it's a groove in the rock, not a runnel.'

'I'd call that a notch, not a col,' and so on. The English language has so much variation even when it comes to specialist topics like mountaineering.

Still, even within a few short weeks, we felt as if we'd made a good start on the book. On one of my early outings, as I was descending a steep mountain, I noticed a family below on the path. They'd stopped on a small outcrop of rock, and the father stood assessing the scene on his map. Almost instinctively, I got my camera out and snapped a picture of him. A dramatic backdrop of craggy buttresses with a mountain hut and a deep blue sky made me feel sure that I'd captured a suitable image for the front cover of the book. After an excited but uncertain wait, we got the slides back from the developers, and I was even more jubilant and confident that I'd got the cover shot.

Drawing the maps was a challenging and time-consuming process and one that we tended to put off as long as possible. Because the terrain of the Julian Alps is exceptionally steep, the contour lines on the maps are so tight and numerous that it makes drawing them virtually impossible. However, we now had enough material to send to Jonathan and our editor. We spent an anxious few days waiting for their feedback and distracted ourselves swimming at Bled and enjoying coffee and cake in the friendly lakeside bars.

We were both elated on the day we received Jonathan's email informing us that we were on the right track. Although we'd sent several choices of photo, he'd chosen my 'man with map' image for the front cover. The editor also accepted our concerns regarding the problem with the contour lines and decided they could use colour shading to show the height differences on the steeper peaks.

Perhaps even more than Justi, I felt very satisfied with our new project. The guidebook gave me something to focus on, and even though I knew it would make virtually no difference to our precarious finances, it still made me feel like I was somehow contributing. After years of using guidebooks ourselves, it felt like we were now giving something back to the mountaineering community. However, it wouldn't be for another seven years that guidebook writing paid us back in an unexpected and slightly abstract way. But that, as they say, is another story…

One morning, as we were about to leave for another day in the mountains, Janez and Ana arrived to spend the weekend at their apartment on the ground floor.

'You go to the mountains a lot,' Ana remarked as we loaded our rucksacks into the car.

'Well, we're actually writing a book about the Julian Alps,' Justi said and added, 'I must say that we feel a bit embarrassed to be doing it.'

'Why are you embarrassed?' asked Janez, sounding surprised.

'Well, these are your mountains, and we aren't Slovenes.'

'Ha, but the British have always been explorers. It's just what you do.'

We laughed but recognised he did have a point. A plaque on a house nearby stated that Sir Humphrey Davy, inventor of the miners' safety lamp, had once stayed there on his travels. And only recently, TV crews had arrived in the village to film an episode of *A Place in the Sun* because a Brit had bought a house there. Whether looking for an adventure, travelling or migrating for work and a new life, Brits have always been explorers in one way or another.

Not long after this, Janez introduced us to a friend of his, Jože, who was a mountain guide. We gleaned a lot of useful information and advice regarding routes and off-the-beaten-track, alternative paths. Like so many other Slovenes that we've met over the years, all of whom have willingly shared their expert local knowledge, we'll always appreciate Janez and Jože's help during those early guidebook-writing days.

It was now the end of the school summer holiday, and Justi settled into her new job. She immediately noticed that the general behaviour and discipline of the children was better than it had been in Podpetek. It wasn't that the attitude of the kids in Podpetek was particularly bad, but it could have been better. She put this down to the children's respect for the firm but very fair leadership of the headteacher, Polona.

Although Justi had had misgivings about spending 30 minutes each way in the car, her commute up and down the valley was a stunningly scenic drive. As the summer came to a close, autumn turned the valley into a kaleidoscope of rich colour. Autumn crocuses filled the meadows, and the warm orange and gold of the trees contrasted perfectly with the impossibly blue alpine skies. The tourist season was over, and the main road through the valley became quiet. Driving to work in such surroundings with hardly any other traffic would have been very enjoyable, but the Chariot had developed problems.

Over the year, we'd put a lot of miles on the old car's clock. A knocking from the front wheels had become increasingly loud; large pockets of rust had rapidly formed, and various electrical problems had developed. It seemed that every time we managed to put aside a small cushion of savings, the car greedily demanded it. When the electric passenger window dropped into the door and refused to show itself again, it was the last straw. We knew we'd have to replace the Great White Chariot but wondered how we would manage to get a loan from our Slovene bank, having only been in the country for a year. Our concerns were confirmed when the bank declined our application. The smiling bank official told us that we could apply again in another twelve months and assured us that we'd likely be successful next time.

This didn't solve our immediate problem, though. Once again, my dad came up trumps. Without asking, he happily suggested, in fact insisted, that he could lend us enough to buy a decent used car and that we could pay him back over a year. My father had a strong dislike of the high interest rates asked from banks and credit companies at the time, so he refused to accept any interest from us.

We were very grateful and immediately began to look locally for a used car as having an open window in the Chariot wasn't ideal. It wasn't that we saw it as a security issue; like in the Scottish Highlands, we often left the car unlocked without feeling any concern that it would be stolen. In any case, the English registration and right-hand drive would have made it easily traceable. The weather was fine too, but when Justi left for work at 6.30 a.m. each day, the blast of alpine air was a bit too fresh and noisy as she drove down the valley in the windowless Chariot.

We mentioned our need to a local mechanic who had done some work for us.

'*Ja*, no problem. Come back tomorrow, and I will have a nice car for you.'

We were surprised and pleased to receive such a fast and positive response to our request.

'A customer of mine has a Renault Megane they want to sell. It's a good car; I have always serviced it,' he went on.

We no longer needed such a large car, so we reasoned a Megane, or maybe something even smaller, would be a good bet. The next day, we went to see the car, which seemed to be as good as our mechanic had described. However, the asking price of £3,000 was a little more than we were able to pay. We thanked him for showing us and asked him to keep us in mind should anything else come his way.

The next day, we headed into Jesenice to check out the few car dealers and garages in the hope of finding a replacement for the ailing Chariot, which seemed to sense its time was up. Apart from its failing electrics and knocking ball joints, its heart—the engine—seemed to be going into cardiac arrest. People stared as the Chariot lurched through the town, coughing and spluttering in despair as though it had suddenly become aware of its impending demise.

We pulled into a Citroën garage that had a few used trade-ins lined up neatly outside. It was a family-run franchise, and a lady, probably mum, glanced up from a pile of papers as we entered. She looked more like a mature, expertly made-up air hostess than a car dealer.

'*Dober dan, kako vam lahko pomagam*? (Good day, how can I help you?)' she asked.

'Hello. We're looking for a second-hand car and wondered if—'

'What was wrong with the Megane?'

'What?' we both asked in amazed unison.

'Er, nothing was wrong with it; it was just a bit too expensive,' I went on, as we both wondered how she could have known about our dealings with a mechanic in a small village twenty kilometres away. At the time, we were the only English people living permanently in the valley, so it seemed that word got around fast in the tightly knit Slovene community.

'I think we might have something for you. My son will show you some vehicles,' she said.

We followed her son, a huge, bearded man probably in his late 30s with a thick mop of dark hair, out onto the garage forecourt. He also spoke English fluently, and when he discovered our price range, took us to view the last two cars in the line-up of about fifteen. The first was a tired-looking Fiat saloon with a disturbingly high mileage, but the last in the row looked a better proposition. It was a clean, low-mileage Daewoo Lanos hatchback with a bright metallic blue paint job. And at £2,500, it was in our price range.

After a short test drive, we decided that the Lanos was the car for us. Handing over the money was the only easy part of becoming a vehicle owner. We had to visit government offices in another town to collect official documents which then had to be verified and stamped in another office back in Jesenice before we could 'pass go'. It was like a long-drawn-out treasure hunt that led from one office to another before we finally collected the treasure—a set of green number plates that showed we were the foreign owners of a Slovene car.

With its long shiny bonnet, neat black radiator and rotund rear end, we soon conjured up an imaginary personality for our new mode of transport. Clearly, Lanos was a medallion-wearing seaside type, endearingly plump, that swaggered about in Bermuda shorts and wore mirrored sunglasses—a sort of 'Danny Devito goes to Mykonos' persona. The last stage of our 'new car day' was the hardest—getting rid of the old one. With Justi following behind in the swanky Lanos, I drove the Chariot to the scrap yard. With eerie and uncanny timing, the Chariot's engine stopped metres before the yard gates, and I coasted to a stop alongside the reception hut just inside the entrance. I handed over the official scrap-verification documents to a man behind the sliding desk window who then handed me a receipt.

Outside, five or six men, who seemed to have appeared from nowhere, stood around the Chariot eagerly looking inside.

'Hey, English, how you drive with wheel on wrong side?' one joked as another jumped inside and gripped the steering wheel as if driving a race car.

'Well, you're welcome to try for yourself. Here's the key,' I replied, adding, 'if you can start it,' under my breath.

Another man opened the bonnet and started taking the battery out while for some strange sentimental reason I automatically removed the number plates to take home. I still have them.

Justi had been watching from the smug-looking Lanos, and as I got in the passenger seat, I noticed she was crying.

'They're like a wake of vultures descending on a carcass,' she sobbed as the men opened the Chariot's doors and began removing various bits.

'Well, you know they're doing a great job of recycling. It's just added interest for them today having a right-hand drive to work on,' I said, trying to cheer her up.

We both felt sad, though; the Chariot had been a big part of our Slovene adventure, and well, if you give things a name, they sometimes take on an identity you can come to appreciate and even love. The Chariot had brought us to Slovenia safely with nearly all our worldly goods, and it had done its job well.

Chapter 19 Snapshots and Saints

Autumn in the north-west of Slovenia was as beautiful as in Podpetek, but the colours were even more vibrant. The higher altitude turned the sky a deep gentian blue, and this, in turn, intensified the fiery orange and gold of the turning leaves. A light dusting of early snow on the high tops had me fervently seeking out the best viewpoints in the valley and mountains for the perfect photo.

Justi had settled into her new job and was happy in her work. Many of the things that she'd found stressful during her early teaching days were made easier by familiarity and the experience she'd gained in Podpetek. I continued to record mountain walks for the guidebook, knowing that the high mountain huts were now closing as the main walking season was at an end. Although we had another whole year to complete the walks for the book, we were aware of the short length of the summer trekking season. Soon, a deep blanket of snow would cover the mountain paths and trails, and any work we could do on the book would be limited to drawing maps and planning future walks.

By now, I'd amassed quite a stock of pictures, so I contacted a photo library in the UK to see if they'd be interested in any of my images. After sending a selection of about a hundred, I was delighted to receive an email from them saying they wanted to add half to their stock. Every few weeks, I sent more batches of my best slides and waited to see how many, if any, the library might choose. Although I never expected my picture sales to bring in much cash, I was happy to find that, occasionally, a cheque would arrive that helped towards the cost of film and camera equipment.

One afternoon in late November, the snow arrived in the valley. It started as most snowfalls in the Alps—large powdery flakes that drifted gently down from a cold steely grey sky. When we woke the following morning, the insulating silence told us that a significant amount of snow had fallen.

'What's it like out there?' asked Justi, as I peered through the window and tried to make sense of the featureless scene of pure white that was lit by the dim streetlights.

I looked down into the drive, and for a moment, I thought the car had gone. As my perceptions adjusted to this new white world, I could make out a vague car shape as I followed a contour in the thick blanket of snow. A dark wing mirror protruding from the whiteness confirmed my perception.

'I think I'd better get out there quick and start digging if you're going to get to work on time,' I replied, as Justi joined me at the window.

'Bloody hell, where's the car? Where's the road?'

She stared out of the window, her mouth falling open in shock.

'Those orange flashing lights down on the main road must be a snowplough. Let's hope it will come up here soon. You get the kettle on and get ready. I'll dig the car out,' I said as I rummaged in the wardrobe for warm clothes.

I was relieved to see that Janez had left several shovels at the side of the house together with a large aluminium scoop which I used to push the snow off the drive and onto the garden. After locating the car, I imagined I heard a muffled voice, an angry, muffled voice. I carefully shovelled the snow off the roof and bonnet.

'What kinda place d'ya call this? Hey, d'ya thinks I want snow on my best Hawaiian shirt? Drive me to the Italian coast now. I wanna pina colada,' raged Lanos as I brushed the snow from his radiator grill.

Just as I'd cleared the drive to the road, the snowplough went by and deposited a mountain of snow back into the gateway as it swept past. I groaned in frustration, and more frantic digging and scooping ensued as the mound of snow in the garden grew higher and higher.

Justi left for work, and I watched as she disappeared down the road behind a white curtain of spindrift. The snow continued falling almost without a break all day, and an hour before she was due home, I started digging out the drive again so that she could park. This routine continued for the next three days as the snow continued to fall. When it finally stopped, it was more than two metres deep and had reached the level of the rain gutters on the low sloping eaves at the rear of the house. The mound of snow on the lawn had grown to the same depth as the gutters as I'd piled it up, and I could now stand level with the top of the tall garden hedge and look down on the car roofs as they passed on the road.

As the pass is an important one into Austria, both countries cooperate; the ploughs from both sides meet at the top and contrive to keep the road open, except for just a few days each year after an exceptional snowfall or occasionally an avalanche. As the ploughs push the snow towards the side of the road, massive embankments are formed. These can often collapse and cause the roads to narrow alarmingly. To counter this, machines with large rotating blades slice the snow into neat vertical walls two or more metres high on either side of the road. Sometimes, there's so much snow lying that the local authorities use excavators with humongous buckets to scoop it from the roads and pavements and load it into dumper trucks. The trucks, in turn, then tip the snow into the River Sava.

Despite the best efforts of the Slovene road maintenance crews, unusually heavy snowfall can make driving difficult. After a snowstorm, it's as though the landscape has been suddenly transformed, sometimes literally within a few hours. The high walls of snow on the side of the road mean visibility is reduced at bends and junctions. The authorities do a great job, and even in the alpine areas, the roads are kept open, and life goes on. We found it surprisingly easy to adjust mentally to the rapid seasonal change of the Slovenian winter. Perhaps the most difficult thing was the length of the winters and knowing that the same snow that fell in November was likely to be still lying even into April.

Each day, I put on my skis or snowshoes to cross the sloping meadows to reach the shops in Kranjska Gora. When the sun shone, it was a winter wonderland. The pine trees hung heavy in their white winter robes, and the mountains looked like they'd been coated with thick cake icing. The town was full of happy skiers and snowboarders; it was going to be a good season for Kranjska Gora.

At the weekends, we would cross-country ski or go for walks in the local hills, wearing snowshoes. One day, while we were walking along a high track above the valley, we started chatting to a Slovene couple who were also out enjoying the deep snow and winter sun. Jure and Neža lived in a small village south of Ljubljana and were having a weekend break in Kranjska Gora. They both spoke excellent English and were keen to have a chance to practise it with native speakers.

Right from the start, we enjoyed their company, and the feeling was obviously mutual as they invited us to have dinner with them in the evening. Over the following years, we were to meet up with Jure and Neža for walks, bike rides and meals together. It was a chance meeting that typified the friendly nature of the Slovene people who take great pleasure in sharing their landscape and national food with strangers.

Although the Slovenes celebrate Christmas Day on December 25th, as in most Western countries where Christianity is the dominant religion, their other winter traditions differ from those in the UK. During the first week in December in many European alpine countries, men dress up as horned demons and don horrific masks. The unique costumes of our village include goat skins and sheep fleeces with fanged masks topped with long twisted horns. Brass and copper cowbells are worn around the waist, and these are shaken and jangled loudly for extra effect. Many of these costumes are very old and handed down through the generations.

The monsters patrol the village streets in the evening and pounce on any unfortunate local they come across. They then make them kneel and confess to any bad behaviour they may have committed during the year. The punishment usually involves having their face blacked with charcoal or being rolled in the snow. In the German-speaking countries, the demons are known by the name *Krampusse* and in Slovenia, *parkeljni*.

We'd also heard that Santa Claus, the benevolent Saint Nicholas, or Miklavs (pronounced Mick-louse, more or less) in Slovenia, visited the local children on December 6th. We were intrigued to learn that, although he was allegedly a friendly chap and would arrive with an angel—his helpful assistant—a group of *parkeljni* would accompany him. He would ask each child to sing or recite a poem to him, and if he were pleased with the kid's rendition, then all would be dandy, and the child would receive a small gift. But if the kid's musical or literary skills didn't quite cut the mustard for Miklavs, then the (presumably) terrified kid would be handed over to the Satan squad.

To us, this sounded more interesting than a UK Santa's role, which might involve a tentative enquiry regarding a child's behaviour and a couple of 'Yo ho hos' followed by asking what mega-expensive item of temporary distraction they'd like their parents to second-mortgage the house for.

So, on the evening of December 6th, along with most of the locals, we filed into a dimly lit room above the local fire station, which served as a village community hall, to meet the Slovene Santa. We took seats near the back of the room as it began to fill with parents and children, some of whom nervously clutched pieces of paper with their songs, stories and poems written on them. The babble of excited voices in the room suddenly hushed as a commotion downstairs announced the arrival of Miklavs. Everyone, including the adults, smiled and let out an appreciative gasp of wonder as the tall figure of a white-haired and -bearded Miklavs entered the room, holding a long staff in one hand and a large red book in the other.

He was dressed in a splendid white robe and mitre hat, both trimmed with gold silk. His angel, a young lady, also dressed in white and with silver curly tresses, had her face painted gold. She looked a vision of angelic virtue, and even the Doc Martin boots I noticed she was wearing added to her surreal appearance.

Then everyone, including the adults again, drew in a gasp of shock and horror as the demon crew came into the room. The red-robed, horned devils rattled chains and roared fiercely at any kid who wasn't by now hiding behind their parents in abject fear. A few kids screamed excitedly; one or two tough nuts (there are always one or two, aren't there?) stood their ground and, with mock bravado, faced their demons and shouted back, while another one or two wailed and sobbed in pitiful fright.

With their dramatic entrance routine over, the masked *parkeljni* lined up behind Miklavs who was now sitting at a table facing the room and opening his big red book of children's names. The book also contained an annual report on the character and virtues of each kid. One by one, he called the children out to the front so that they could recite their piece while the red devils hovered menacingly in the background, ready to swoop. As each child finished and waited for the verdict, Miklavs would pause, adding game-show effect before giving the nod to his angel who would hand the kid a present. Or not...

Occasionally, after scrutinising his book, Miklavs would give the nod to the brute squad who would terrorise the kid by daubing charcoal on their face while rattling their chains and bells with demonic fervour. After the torment was over, the kid would then receive a present anyway, and it would invariably end in smiles. For one or two, though, it ended in tears. One poor nervous child stopped reciting their poem in mid-verse and started bawling loudly, and no matter how much Miklavs and his angel tried to placate the stricken six-year-old, the tears kept flowing. Another kid gripped her parent's leg like a whelk, refusing to walk the longest of walks and face Miklavs, while the embarrassed dad tried to prise her off and persuade her that the Beelzebub boys were a decent bunch.

By the end of the evening, every child had received a small gift, and the parents helped themselves to the delicious, homemade snacks and drinks that always accompany village events in Slovenia. As we headed back up the road to our apartment, we chatted about what we'd just witnessed.

'Those *parkeljni* really did appear scary, even to me, so I can only imagine what a small child would make of them,' I said.

'I can imagine some kids being traumatised, but maybe the shared fear and apprehension all the kids face together might have a positive effect,' she said thoughtfully.

'How d'you mean?'

'Well, for most of us in Europe these days, our lives don't include much of the unexpected any more. Our lives are much more controlled and made safe. These kids might be learning how to deal with the fear and uncertainty that our ancestors would have experienced and learned from.'

We both agreed that it was all done in an atmosphere of fun and celebration, and having talked about it with several Slovene friends, they all remembered their Miklavs experience with great fondness, and no one knew of anyone who was permanently traumatised by the bearded saint and his contingent of devils.

Chapter 20 Health

Since we'd arrived in Slovenia, Justi had had access to the Slovene health system, made possible through her job. Each month, a certain amount of money was deducted from her salary to pay for it. For me, though, not being a part of the employment system meant that I wasn't covered. We certainly didn't have any spare money for private health care, so any accident or illness that I might incur would likely involve a sum of money that we could never repay. Also, because I'm a long-term type I (insulin-dependent) diabetic, it became imperative that we found a way for me to get some health cover. Type I diabetes is an expensive disease to own. The insulin and accompanying paraphernalia such as blood-test kits and diagnostic-test strips don't come cheap.

I'd managed to bring a good supply of insulin with me when we first arrived in Podpetek. Keeping active and exercising daily had meant I'd been able to reduce the amount I needed to inject, so I'd eked out my estimated eight-months' supply to last the year. On our summer trip to Scotland, I'd been able to see my old GP who kindly issued me with a prescription for another six-months' supply. He told me that it would be the last time he could do this unless we planned to return to his Highland practice within that time. As my insulin supply began to run out, we searched desperately for a way to find me health cover.

School colleagues had told Justi that it might be possible to add me to her standard health cover as a family member, for an affordable extra fee. So, on a cold January day, we went to the town council offices that dealt with the Slovene health insurance scheme. We sat down outside an office in a long corridor with a brightly polished floor as Justi checked through all the paperwork she thought we'd need to get me my health cover. Through the frosted glass door of the office, I could see the shape of an extraordinarily large person behind a desk, silhouetted against a window.

'OK, that's everything,' said Justi as she stood up.

We knocked on the door and entered the office. An enormous Slovene lady looked up at us with a somewhat disinterested look.

'Er, *dober dan*,' Justi started then continued in Slovene, explaining that our language skills were unfortunately not good enough to discuss insurance matters. 'Do you speak English?' she finished.

The lady stared coldly at Justi for a moment before making a barely perceptible nod. 'A little.'

We sat down at the desk while Justi spoke clearly about our dilemma and gently pushed all her paperwork across the desk to her. She then asked if it was true that I could be added to her insurance as a member of her family.

'*Ne*,' came the answer.

'No? Why not?' asked Justi.

'He needs to be a resident of Slovenia to get health care.'

'He lives with me. Doesn't that make him a resident?'

'*Ne*.'

'Well, how can he become a resident?'

'He must have a health insurance document.'

'What?'

'You must show a health insurance document; then he can be resident...maybe.'

'But that's why we're here. We want health insurance.'

'*Ne*. He must be resident!'

It was obvious this Catch 22 impasse was going nowhere, so Justi tried another angle of attack.

'OK, if we can prove to you that he lives with me here in Slovenia, will that help him get insurance?'

Although her face was expressionless, the big lady seemed to mull this over for a moment before replying, '*Ne*,' and with that, she handed Justi her documents back to emphasise that the interview was over. She hadn't made any eye contact with me at all; it was evident she saw me as a problem and would only deal with Justi as she was the one who had a Slovene work permit and the right to residency.

'We'll be back,' said Justi, and I followed behind her as she headed for the door. Walking down the corridor, Justi aired her frustration.

'*Ne, ne, ne, ne*! She's like a bloody sea wall. My questions just bounced off her.'

'What can we do now?' I asked as I sensed she had something in mind.

'We'll get our tenancy agreement and also ask Janez for a letter stating that we both live in his house.'

'Hmm, but the sea-wall lady said she wouldn't accept proof of our living together.'

'Ah, but I was talking to Janez the other day, and he told me he was a barrister. He's only recently retired, so surely a letter from him, hopefully on headed paper, should help.'

Within a week, we were back in the council office sitting in front of our unhelpful nemesis. Justi handed her our tenancy agreement papers then produced her pièce de résistance, an impressive headed letter that Janez had been happy to supply. Justi was confident that his letter, written in Slovene, would be enough to show that we were living together permanently in Slovenia.

The sea-wall woman read the letter then, looking up at Justi, flipped it dismissively back across the desk and said, '*Ne.*'

'What do you mean, "*Ne*"? Look, my husband has diabetes. He will die unless we get health insurance!'

Tears of anguish, frustration and genuine worry for my health welled up in her eyes. Sea-wall woman sat looking silently and impassively at Justi. She wouldn't be breached this day.

'What are we going to do?' sobbed Justi in the car as we made our way home.

'We'll think of something. I've still got enough insulin for another week or so,' I said, trying to reassure her that my death wasn't so imminent. Over the next few days, we tried in vain to come up with a solution. Then one evening, as I finally got around to unpacking a box of books that had been put aside since we'd moved in the summer, a piece of paper dropped out of one and spun to the floor.

'What's that you dropped?' Justi asked.

'It's just an old E111 form of mine, 1984. I probably got it when I went on my first climbing trip to the French Alps.' (Before the European Health Card, this form entitled people travelling abroad to free health care on a reciprocal rights basis.)

'Hmm, I wonder… Don't throw it away; pass it here,' said Justi.

The next day, we were back in the council office, sitting opposite the lady who liked to say '*Ne*'.

'OK,' said Justi, 'I think I have what you need,' and assertively handed my tattered, twenty-year-out-of-date, void and invalid E111 to Mrs Sea Wall. 'This is his British health certificate, and now I would like him to have a new Slovene one, please.'

Mrs Sea Wall scrutinised the delicately thin, ancient scrap of paper. After what seemed like an eternity, she looked up and said in a slightly more animated tone, '*Ja*...this is good.'

She seemed oddly pleased with the old E111 and stared at it with interest before carefully filing it away like an avid stamp collector who'd just acquired a Victorian Penny Black.

Justi and I glanced at each other in astonishment, overjoyed that we'd made a breakthrough in our insurance dilemma. After that, Mrs Sea Wall seemed to relent a little and told Justi, still without acknowledging my presence, that I should return tomorrow to collect my residency permit. As soon as I'd signed it, Justi could apply to have me included on her health insurance for a small monthly top-up fee, and it should take no longer than a week to process.

Feeling jubilant, we thanked her and left the office quickly and silently in case she changed her mind. Once in the car, we erupted into excited conversation as we headed home, trying to make sense of the events that had just unfolded.

'What did you make of that?' I spluttered while Justi just shook her head, looking dazed and staring straight ahead.

'Extraordinary,' she said, sounding uncharacteristically stupefied. 'I certainly didn't expect that old document would make her defences crumble.'

With Slovenia expecting to join the EU in May, it was experiencing a time of turmoil and change throughout all its national and local institutions. As far as we knew, we were the first Brits to be living permanently in the valley, and our presence often confused the staff of the government departments we had to deal with.

We'd found many of the council offices we'd had to visit in Slovenia to be overly bureaucratic, and we wondered if that was an influence from its not-so-distant communist past.

Like many local office staff at the time, our Mrs Sea Wall seemed to be bound by her narrow departmental confines. I expected that she wouldn't have deviated from her duties by suggesting to us other options or possibilities even if they'd existed.

It wasn't just government departments. We'd found that the amount of paperwork and documentation needed for even simple transactions, such as returning a small item bought in error at a shop, usually involved triplicate papers and signatures. It seemed that Mrs Sea Wall was only content when she had an official document to stamp and file away. The fact that my ancient, and undoubtedly invalid, E111 ticked her boxes, was fine with us.

Whether you're a resident with health cover or not, the health care system in Slovenia is excellent. Justi had been impressed to discover that, in addition to having your own GP, every woman has access to a personal gynaecologist. This takes the pressure off GPs as well as adding a high level of care. As soon as I received my health care cover and residency permit, I was able to have regular check-ups at the hospital's diabetic clinic.

While the care and specialist medical facilities in Slovenia can be state-of-the-art, the appointments system, like many of the state-run services, seemed to us archaic and unnecessarily complex—perhaps another bureaucratic hangover from communist times. It took us several visits to the doctor's and outpatient clinics before we got a grasp on the order of things. For example, if you have an appointment to see your doctor at 10 a.m., don't expect to waltz in on time and be shown through to the GP's room by a smiling receptionist. Regardless of what time your appointment is, you'll likely sit in a corridor, possibly with ten or more patients, and wait for a locked door at one end to be opened by a receptionist or nurse. As soon as the door is opened, everyone will leap up, elbowing each other out of the way to hand in their electronic health insurance card. Don't be fooled by that fragile, sweet old lady, who seems to be at death's door. She'll break your ribs.

As soon as all the cards are handed in, everyone returns to their seat calmly, and it's all smiles and small talk again. Some Slovene cultural habits may seem unfathomable to the British, especially regarding the orderly queue. But if the Slovenes lack of regard for queuing causes consternation to a Brit, they counter this and disarm you in other ways. For example, every patient, stranger or not, will announce their arrival and departure to all in the waiting room with a cheery *Dober dan* and *Nasvidenje* (goodbye).

The whole appointment procedure can be even more intimidating at a busy hospital. At the hospital clinic, you'll queue to see a receptionist and then be handed one or more sheets of paper covered in peel-off labels to be handed in to various laboratories. When you've finally worked out which laboratories you need to visit and provided the labels, which are then stuck to the sample pots of whatever you've given, you go through the rigmarole as above to see the doctor on duty. Only since 2016 has this system begun to change and modernise, at least in some of the hospitals.

Our local GP, Janko, had become a friend. One of his hobbies had been to record local weather events. Justi had helped to collect and log all the data to his computer, and Janko had kindly assisted us with some research on our guidebook. I won't forget, nor will Justi ever let me, that, on one particular occasion, Janko helped save my life.

Like most diabetics, occasionally my blood glucose level will drop too low (a hypoglycaemic reaction or hypo) if I haven't matched my insulin intake to the amount of food and exercise I've had. Normally, I recognise this and quickly remedy the situation by eating or drinking something sweet enough to bring my sugar level back up. But on two incidents (so far) in my life, my blood glucose level has dropped so low that I became comatose.

The first time this happened, in the early 1980s, I was staying at a mountain hut in the Ogwen Valley in North Wales. I'd hitched there with a friend, and we'd spent a glorious week rock climbing and walking in the hills. I'd woken early, planning to make breakfast and get out on the crags again for the last day of our trip. I took my insulin injection then reclined back in my bunk, thinking I'd just have an extra minute or two of blissful relaxation before I began my chores. The next thing I knew, I was being brought out of a coma in Gynwedd hospital near the coast.

My pal had woken to find me unconscious in my bunk and, being unable to wake me, had walked a kilometre or so to the nearest building, which happened to be a mountain rescue post. They immediately requested an ambulance and, accompanied by my friend, I was whisked to hospital. I suppose it may seem bizarre that, in all the time I've spent in the mountains, the only time I've ever needed the assistance of a mountain rescue team was when I was still tucked up in bed.

My friend had acted fast and may even have saved my life, so I suppose I must forgive him for not bringing my shoes or trousers in the ambulance. Wearing my long johns, a threadbare pullover and a pair of white surgical clogs two sizes too big that the hospital had given me, I hitchhiked back to the Ogwen Valley. I've often mused as to why someone would stop and provide a lift for such a dubiously dressed person, but they did. Maybe it says something about 1980s fashion. By midday, my friend and I were back on the crags, scaling a very severe rock climb. The audacity and ignorance of youth, I suppose.

The second time I fell into a coma was in Slovenia when I wasn't so youthful and should have known better. Youth may be wasted on the young, but wisdom isn't a natural consequence of getting older either. I'd signed up for an amateur cycle race in Italy, a one-day sportive event that involved 230 kilometres of hilly riding. I'd been managing to cycle between 300 and 400 kilometres per week in my training but, as the race day approached, I wanted to emulate a route that would be comparable to the actual event. I plotted a special ride and put my plan into action the following morning.

I cycled from our village across the border to Austria and over the Nassfeld Pass into Italy. My ride continued over the Predel Pass and back into Slovenia, followed by climbing the Vršič Pass that brought me back to Kranjska Gora. It was a good 200-kilometre ride and involved considerably more climbing than the sportive itself, so I felt tired but pleased when I got back to the apartment late in the afternoon.

The following morning, I'd planned to do another training ride, but it wasn't to be. Justi had already left for work, and I was anxious to get my breakfast and be on my way. Looking out of the window, I lost enthusiasm when I saw heavy drops of rain begin to fall. I decided to have a rest day and took my dose of insulin then made the same mistake I'd done twenty years previously. Feeling suddenly tired, I sat down on the sofa to give myself a few minutes before I'd start to make my breakfast.

Justi was expecting to have a long day in work, but a meeting planned in the late afternoon was cancelled, so she returned home about 2 p.m. She found me lying on the sofa, comatose, and was unable to wake me. My breathing was very shallow. Smearing a spoon with jam on the inside of my mouth, she tried to get some glucose into my system, but I began to choke. When a few minutes later there was still no response, Justi worried that it wasn't just a hypo but that I'd had a stroke. She phoned Janko, who left work and came to our apartment immediately.

He gave me an injection of glucose, but it didn't prompt any change. Justi could sense by Janko's uncharacteristically serious demeanour that all was not well. He phoned for an ambulance then explained to Justi that my recent exercise had probably depleted my glycogen stores to a very low point, and I was unable to stimulate enough response in my muscles and circulatory system to distribute the glucose effectively. They both rushed out onto the balcony when they heard the ambulance screaming up the pass but were exasperated to see that it had turned on a track across the meadows and was heading in the wrong direction. Janko quickly pulled out his phone to inform them of their error, and he came back inside to try injecting me with more glucose. Justi stayed on the balcony to redirect the ambulance by waving frantically.

By the time the ambulance medics arrived in our apartment, the glucose injections had begun to have an effect, and with surprising speed, I came out of the coma. As in Wales, I was no worse for wear and was just initially confused as to what people in orange overalls were doing in the room. I felt like I'd had a deep, relaxing sleep and even glanced from my sickbed sofa out of the window, wondering if the rain had stopped so I could still get a ride in.

However, even if still not exactly wise, I knew better than to start filling my water bottle and held Justi tightly as she told me how she'd thought my number was up. I realised just how lucky I'd been when she explained how her meeting had been cancelled and she'd returned home early. Janko confirmed that I would have died, or at least suffered serious complications, if I'd been left for much longer without medical help.

Chapter 21 Making New Friends—and Losing an Old One

As the winter snows came to an end, a band of bright green growth that rose from the valley floor up the mountainsides heralded spring in the valley. By the end of each day, this new forest growth appeared noticeably higher. We'd witnessed a reverse of this phenomenon the previous autumn when the warm red and gold colours of the season swept down the mountains to the valley floor.

A common sight in early spring is that of local people wandering across the meadows with a bag and a pair of scissors. At first, we wondered what on earth they were doing, picking something out of what appeared to be simply grass. We eventually discovered that they were stooping to cut and collect the young leaves of dandelions which are particularly nutritious and the first fresh greens of the year. They're used as the main ingredient in a delicious, early-season salad that usually includes hardboiled eggs, diced boiled potatoes and maybe some crispy smoked bacon. Primrose flowers are also often added to this popular spring dish.

In May 2004, Slovenia officially became a member state of the European Union, and we were intrigued to hear that the moment was to be celebrated on the mountain Tromeja, which means Three Borders, near Kranjska Gora. It would have been hard to find a more symbolic place for the occasion as on its summit meet not only three countries—Slovenia, Italy and Austria—but also the three great cultures and language families of Europe—Slavic, Romance and Germanic.

The prime minister of Slovenia, along with the Austrian chancellor and the deputy prime minister of Italy (Mr Berlusconi had mistakenly made his way to Slovakia. Only kidding, he was ill at the time) were to attend the event, along with a sizeable crowd of locals from each country. We made our way to the little village of Rateče at the foot of the mountain. A steep forest road leads almost to the top from there, and a good number of people had already begun the steady hike up when we arrived. A series of minibuses had been laid on by the local authorities to ferry people up the road, but we chose to walk as it was a hill we hoped to include in our guidebook and so wanted to find out more about it. A minibus passed, its passengers dressed in smart uniforms and clutching various musical instruments, a large man taking up two seats as he balanced a massive tuba in front of him.

'The local brass band,' Justi commented.

A few minutes later, we side-stepped quickly off the road as a convoy of gleaming four-wheel drive vehicles with darkened passenger windows swept past.

'And that must be Anton Rop, the Slovenian prime minister. They all had Ljubljana registration plates,' I noted as we stepped back onto the road, taking care to check the coast was now clear.

Not long before we reached the top, another convoy of shiny 4x4s passed, this time with Austrian number plates. As they went by, we saw that one of the dignitaries had his window wound down and was leaning out, waving and smiling to the people hiking up the track.

'Hmm, d'you think that's the Austrian chancellor?' I asked. 'He seems pretty laid back and unconcerned about security if it is.'

'No, that's Jörg Haider, the Austrian governor of Carinthia. Remember, we saw his picture in the paper?'

Carinthia is the region of Austria that lies on the other side of the pass, and we'd heard Haider's name mentioned several times, even in the international papers. He was a politician who courted controversy and media attention with his extreme views on many topical subjects and had been accused of having Nazi sympathies and an anti-Semite stance. The success of his far-right political party had caused several EU member states to force diplomatic sanctions against Austria a few years before.

We joined the several thousand people gathered on the summit of the hill and listened to the surprisingly moving speeches of the political leaders followed by the brass band playing the inevitably jovial local oompah tunes. However, it was the controversial Dr Jörg Haider who stole the show; his charismatic demeanour drew the crowd's attention like a magnet. In spite of his questionable politics, it was easy to see why he had such a following.

He'd gained much of his popularity by portraying himself as a family man who spoke up for hard-working families. A few years later, we were shocked to see his death reported on the TV news. According to the report, he'd crashed his car while speeding with a blood alcohol level over three times the limit, having not long left a local gay bar.

During the late spring and summer, Justi and I spent most of our time exploring the Julian Alps, taking photographs and recording the walks for our guidebook. Cliché it may be, but another day in our office usually meant hiking the incredibly beautiful mountains and valleys under sunny azure skies, either together or alone. Sometimes, I would follow a high trail and stay overnight in a hut while Justi researched a valley walk or lower hill with Bryn as her companion. It was on one particular hill walk we'd arranged to do together that we saw Bryn finally yielding to his great old age.

Although he was now fifteen years old, he still showed willing— if not exactly bounding enthusiasm—to join us on every outing we made. The walk we'd chosen to do on this occasion wasn't long, but it did involve a steep ascent through a forest to reach a high alpine pasture. As we emerged from the woods onto the grassy summit slopes, we saw that something was wrong with Bryn. He almost always walked a few metres ahead of us but was now lagging far behind. We turned to see him moving uncharacteristically slowly, and rather than hurrying to catch us up as we waited for him, he stopped.

'C'mon, fella,' I said, slapping my leg and expecting him to make his usual dash as I opened my rucksack to fish out a treat for him.

Although he tried, he just wasn't able to make any more headway on the steep path. As we sat with him while he lapped some water and ate his treats, we saw a sad, almost resigned, look in his eyes that we'd never seen before.

During the previous week, he'd enjoyed long valley walks with Justi and hadn't shown any signs of being overly tired or in any discomfort. Today, it was different, and it was heart-wrenching to see our old friend of countless hill trips no longer able to lead us to another summit.

Having rested, we turned around and made our way slowly down through the forest with Bryn beside us. It was to be his last hill walk. As the summer advanced, he became much slower, and a short walk across the meadows opposite the house became his daily routine. He was now content to while away the warmer days sleeping on the apartment balcony for long periods.

*****

One morning, while Justi and I were having breakfast on the balcony, we noticed an elderly lady in the garden.

'I wonder if she's looking for Janez and Ana,' Justi said.

'*Dober dan, ali lahko pomagam*? (Hello, can I help you?)' I asked, leaning over the balcony rail, eager to practise my Slovene.

'Ah, hello, you must be Roy and Justi. Yes?' she replied in faultless English, deflating any hopes that my Slovene might sound at least good enough to disguise my British origins for a nano-second.

'Er...yes, that's right,' we replied, puzzled as to who this kind-faced lady was.

'My name is Marjeta. I live in the village.'

'Please, would you like to come in for some tea or coffee?' we suggested, still puzzled as to our visitor's interest in us.

Over coffee, Marjeta explained that she had a cousin called Jure and that we'd met him while he was on holiday in Kranjska Gora. He'd told her about his meeting with the English couple who now lived in her village and suggested that Marjeta should visit us to practise her language skills.

We instantly recalled our meeting with Jure and his wife, Neža. We'd been fortunate to have experienced several serendipitous encounters like this since we'd arrived in the country. Making social contacts and connections, whether for friendship or business, seemed very much how life in Slovenia operated. We'd found that it was usually the younger folk in Slovenia that had the best English skills, so we were surprised that Marjeta, in her 70s, spoke so fluently. We were even more amazed when she explained that she'd learned English through years of devoted listening to the BBC World Service radio programme, *London Calling.*

Marjeta was to become a close friend who would often drop by for a coffee and informed us of any local events or happenings in the village. She invited Justi to join her each week with the village ladies at the local sewing circle which was held in the dimly lit community room above the fire station. The delicate embroidery and exquisite lacework they produced was stunning, considering the lack of lighting. One lady who produced some of the most skilful and artistic work was also the oldest of the group. Her name was Zora and, although well into her 80s and no longer able to get about easily, she rarely missed an evening to work and chat with the sewing ladies.

Justi learned the basic techniques of embroidery from them, and in return, she shared her patchwork skills. She was fascinated to learn that the way she'd been taught to knit by Betty at about four years old was completely different from the way the local ladies did it, yet the resulting stitches were identical.

She also hoped to improve her Slovene but soon realised that the ladies spoke in a local dialect that made getting to grips with the language even harder. The sewing circle evenings often involved a lot of raucous laughter and gossip as it was a weekly opportunity for many of the women to have a change of scene during the long dark winter evenings. Despite the language difficulties, Justi enjoyed the company and skills of the crafty old ladies.

Next door to our apartment was a traditional farmhouse where three generations of a well-loved and respected family lived. They owned and worked a strip of land on the meadows across the road. The matriarch was an old lady who, like Zora, was in her late 80s. Despite being almost bent double after a lifetime of farm work, she would tend the fertile patch every day during the summer. We would watch her anxiously from the balcony, afraid that she would fall as she made the short journey past the barn and across the road. Forward progress was obviously a considerable effort, and she grasped her walking sticks tightly, pausing for rest at every other step. As soon as she set foot in her field, her struggles seemed to lessen. She became more at ease as she relaxed into her bent posture and began to work.

She weeded the land for hours, turning the soil and clearing small stones. Later in the summer, she carried a large bladed knife to cut and gather baskets of vegetables, beans and flowers. Sometimes, when an afternoon storm brewed suddenly with little warning, Justi rushed out with an umbrella and helped her across the road as the heavens opened. Her husband was probably a few years older, and he also worked the vegetable strip every day and still cut the meadow hay with a scythe. He too was permanently hunched over from the repetitive work. Although he didn't speak any English, he always exchanged a few friendly words whenever we met.

On one occasion, while having a tea break as I trimmed the garden hedge, he sat with me and told me about the one time in his life when he'd been forced to leave the family farm. With a combination of mimes, animated gesticulations and emphasis on key words, I was able to understand his harrowing story. It was during WW2, and he'd been taken prisoner and transported to Russia where he'd been interred in a gulag for several years. His eyes shone bright, and his face lit up as he recalled the happiness he'd felt when he'd finally been released and returned to his home in Slovenia. From that day on, he said, he never wanted to leave the farm again.

Towards the end of the summer, the whole extended family, which included relatives from nearby villages, would be out in the field, harvesting the potatoes and raking in the hay. The sweet-smelling, dry grass and flowers would be loaded onto the wooden beams of the drying racks, called *kozolec*, that stand in the meadows. The *kozolec* is an iconic piece of Slovenian pastoral architecture, and homesick Slovenians sometimes think about these ancient vernacular structures to remind them of their homeland.

The old man's son climbed up the racks and sat balanced across a beam while his sons hefted the hay up to him with pitchforks. He then carefully and evenly loaded it onto the wooden beams to be dried in the warm air before storing it in the barn to feed the cattle. All these family jobs entailed break times that involved baskets of delicious homemade breads, cheeses, pickles, sausages, fruit juices and the inevitable schnapps.

By late summer, we'd completed all the mountain walks that we hoped to include in our guidebook to the Julian Alps. It was now a matter of pulling together all the descriptions, drawing the maps and making photo selections to present to Jonathan and his team by mid-October. We soon discovered that the long walks and hundreds of hours spent climbing steep routes in the mountains had been the easy part. Still, we had a contract to fulfil, so we gritted our teeth and submitted the contents of our book to Jonathan by the deadline. Well, almost.

When we'd emailed all the files and posted all the pictures, we naively believed that we just had to sit back and wait for publication day. In fact, many changes and clarifications had to be made via emails over the winter months. Although this was frustrating at times, the professionalism and skill of our publisher ensured that, once it was published, we were very proud of the book.

During the winter of 2005, Bryn lost the ability to climb or descend the short flight of stairs to our apartment. I had to carry him up and down, but once on level ground, he could waddle slowly along for his usual walk on the track across the snow-covered meadow. Then, one evening in January as he lay in his basket, he suffered a seizure that lasted about ten minutes. When he recovered, he seemed nervous and confused and followed us both around the apartment, his body pressed close to our legs even when we just stood up to put the kettle on. The following morning, we took him to the vet and told her about the seizure and asked whether it could be time to have him put to sleep.

'Well, there's nothing wrong with him; he's just old,' she told us. 'He may experience another seizure, but there's nothing really I can do for him at his age. I don't recommend any investigative techniques and certainly not surgery. If you reach the point where you feel that he's suffering, bring him to me when you're ready, and I'll put him to sleep.'

We took him home, both knowing that the time was fast approaching, or was perhaps already here, to say our goodbyes to Bryn. He perked up a bit, though, and a couple of months went by before we witnessed him having another seizure. As on the previous occasion, when he regained consciousness, he seemed very insecure and frightened. We wondered if he'd experienced any seizures while we'd been out and how terrified he would be if he were alone. That evening, we decided to take him to the vet the following morning for the last time.

It was a beautiful sunny morning in early spring when we drove into the car park outside the surgery. I opened the car, and Bryn squinted at the bright warm sunshine that flooded the rear hatch where he lay. He sniffed the air contentedly, and we sat with him for a few more moments, stroking his soft glossy coat before lifting him gently to the ground.

The vet knew why we'd come; the expressions on our faces told the story. She led us quietly through to her surgery room, and I lifted Bryn onto the table. As always at the vet's, he behaved impeccably.

He trusted us. He went to sleep instantly without any resistance or sound as Justi held and stroked him.

We drove home, unable to control our tears and with the deepest feeling of loss that either of us had felt in a long time. We reasoned that we'd at least been able to give him a last gift, a freedom from the sufferings of extreme old age—a gift that we may never be able to offer to each other. He'd been a faithful and undemanding companion, and it seemed nothing would be quite the same again without him. That afternoon, as we sat drinking tea in our empty-feeling apartment, a thought suddenly overwhelmed me.

'We should have brought his body home and buried him in the garden,' I said as though I'd just realised I'd missed something vitally important and fundamentally obvious.

'I think it'll be too late now, and besides, you'd have to ask Janez and Ana's permission,' Justi replied, slightly startled at my sudden insight.

I phoned the vet and asked if she still had his body.

'Er, *ja*, I do, but wha—'

'OK, I'm going to come and collect him.'

Next, I phoned Janez and Ana as I'd already decided that, even if they didn't give me permission to bury him in the garden, I would make a grave for him in the forest close by. Although initially reluctant, they gave me permission, on the proviso that Bryn's grave must be at least a metre deep. Justi waited outside in the car as the vet led me upstairs to a dark room above the surgery where Bryn's body had been wrapped in a black bin bag and placed in a chest freezer.

'How would you have disposed of the body?' I asked her as I lifted him out.

'Well, the normal procedure is that the bodies are collected and taken to a landfill site where they're covered in quicklime,' she explained.

Although that was no doubt the proper normal procedure, I couldn't bear the thought of Bryn's body receiving so little dignity and veneration. Justi's memory of reclaiming Bryn's body is an image of me running from the surgery door carrying him, with the flustered-looking vet trotting behind as though trying to apprehend me.

In the late afternoon sunshine, we laid him to rest in the garden, wrapped in his favourite blanket, under a shady blossom tree.

Chapter 22 Location, Location, Location

One of the many great things about Slovenia is its location. Being centrally placed in Southern Europe means you're never very far away from other countries, cultures and different landscapes. Austria and Italy are both on the doorstep with Croatia and Hungary also just next door.

While Bryn was still alive, our travelling was limited; our memories of his ordeal with the vet when we arrived in Podpetek made us unwilling to take him across another border. At that time, Croatia wasn't yet a member of the EU, which further complicated matters for a seaside holiday. Sad though we were at Bryn's death, at least it meant that we could now travel further afield.

We'd enjoyed many day trips into nearby Austria and Italy, but now, with the extra freedom, I was able to pack my panniers and head off on a hilly, three-day cycle tour into Austria. In just four kilometres, I reached the border where two Slovene border guards stopped me. I wondered why they were so curious about my bike but soon realised that one of them was a keen cyclist himself. After asking where I was headed, I explained my intended 400-kilometre route to his eager nods of approval. His friend, being more nationalistic, jokingly suggested that I should turn around and cycle through Slovenia instead.

'It eez more beautiful,' he insisted.

Three days later, when I returned through the border, the same guards recognised me and waved me back into Slovenia with a cheer. It had been a lovely trip, and that evening, as I recalled my adventure to Justi, she decided that she would also like to do it. Less than two weeks later, during a half-term break, we cycled past the same two guards on our loaded bikes. The cycle-friendly guard seemed impressed, and perhaps a little jealous, that I was repeating the ride. I promised the patriotic border guard that I'd make my next tour through Slovenia, and so I did.

I rode south through the length of the country and along the Croatian coast to catch a ferry to the beautiful island of Krk. It only took two days riding, testament not only to how small the country is but to how conveniently placed in Europe it is so that it's possible to experience both the mountains and the sea.

On another school holiday, we loaded our bikes onto the car roof rack and drove to Slovakia to see the country whose name is often confused with Slovenia. It's not just US presidents, European politicians and our parents who get mixed up; apparently, the embassy staff from both countries regularly meet to exchange wrongly addressed mail. Slovakia had also recently joined the EU and seemed to be trying to reinvent itself as an outdoor tourist destination. We'd read on the Slovakian tourist board website that it was a country well set up for cycle tourists, and we'd even managed to acquire two maps that showed bike-friendly routes through the whole country.

We had two options planned: Plan A was to drive to a suitable location, park the car and head off on our bikes for a tour through the countryside, staying at B&Bs or cheap hotels. Plan B, in case we couldn't find a place to leave the car for a long period, was to do day rides then move on by car. We arrived in Slovakia after a six-hour drive along the smooth Austrian motorways. First, we visited the beautiful old town centre of the capital city, Bratislava, with its quirky street statues and vibrant coffee bars. We walked alongside the mighty Danube River below the imposing castle that overlooks the city and watched as the long narrow tourist boats battled against the powerful currents.

As evening began to fall, we drove out to the suburbs to find the hostel that we'd booked into. Although the hostel description had sounded fine on the website we'd found, there were only one or two pictures of the interior and none of the outside, except a close-up of the hostel's name on a sign above the entrance. A bright newly built shopping centre stood where we thought our accommodation should be located, so we parked outside and went in to see if anyone could help.

'Let's get a coffee over there at that bar. We could ask the staff about the hostel at the same time,' Justi suggested.

The young man who served us was keen for a chance to practise his English and looked at the address on the hostel booking form that

Justi had printed out before we left home.

'You guys are in the right place, but the hostel's on the opposite side of the highway.' He spoke confidently in an American accent. 'It's in one of those buildings over there,' he said, pointing to what looked like a complex of abandoned apartment blocks.

A tall wire fence stood around the perimeter like a security aid to keep looters out and falling masonry in.

'Are you sure it's in there?' Justi asked worriedly. 'I can't see an entrance or even a light in the building.'

'Yeah, it's down there,' he said, pointing to a dimly lit road just beyond a set of traffic lights. 'You'll see a barrier on the left; that's how you get in.'

Drinking up, we left quickly, not wanting to let it get any darker before we found our accommodation. I drove along the perimeter fence, Justi craning her neck to look up at the dark, empty buildings that might once have been apartments, offices or maybe classrooms of a closed-down college.

'Blimey, they look grim,' she said as I turned down the road and spotted a striped barrier on the left across an entrance into our hostel of horrors.

The barrier remained closed, but thankfully we could see lights in the building just beyond and a group of young folk, perhaps students, standing outside. Above the main door, we recognised the painted sign from the website, declaring the hostel's name. A young man gave us a friendly wave then went inside for a moment before emerging with an older man in blue overalls who came over to our car. Justi wound down her window.

'Hi, we're booked in for one night,' and she showed him our booking confirmation.

'Ah, *ja*, you are the English. Park over there and bring your bikes inside; it is not safe,' he said as he unlocked the barrier.

'OK, we will, but can you show us our room first?' I asked, still feeling very unsure about our choice of accommodation.

Inside, the hostel was bustling with people. The warden first showed us a large canteen room where young student types rubbed shoulders with workmen in overalls. They were seated at long tables, everyone tucking into plates of risotto, pizza and salad. He then showed us to our bunks in a small room that we would share with two other folk. The room was spartan, typical of a basic hostel, and it looked like it had once been used to house nursing staff or had perhaps been part of a student dormitory.

But it was also clean, bright and warm. In the corridor outside, people had lent bikes against the wall, and the warden repeated that we should also bring ours in for safety. Although the exterior and immediate surroundings of the building did look undoubtedly grim, the inside was unexpectedly pleasant. It felt like a safe haven amid a seedy, dilapidated wasteland.

We began to relax and enjoyed a tasty filling meal and several cups of tea, all for an astonishingly low price. After eating, we went to our room to get away from the noise of the dining hall and to plan our route for the next day. By 10.30 p.m., the corridors had become quiet. We'd learned that business and college hours in Slovakia were very similar to Slovenia, so the hostel's clientele of students and working men would be leaving early in the morning. Just one roommate joined us, a student who sounded as though he was trying hard not to disturb us by making his arrival considerate and inconspicuous. He even left the light off as he tiptoed about, but the fumes of alcohol filled the room and betrayed his presence. Stifled Slavic curses followed as he stubbed his toe and missed a step on the ladder to his bunk. As soon as he hit the pillow, he fell into a deep slumber accompanied by a melody of snorts, snuffles and wheezing.

The following morning, we rose early while our student friend slept on and were relieved to see that our bikes and the car were as we'd left them. Even in daylight, the surrounding buildings and parking area still looked depressingly grim but somehow more normal as people left purposefully for work. After a simple breakfast of coffee, bread and jam, we loaded our bikes back onto the car, and the janitor opened the barrier.

Happy to be leaving the city suburbs and driving out into the open countryside, we headed out on a road marked on our map as a recognised cycling route, hoping to find somewhere to park. The first village we came to looked dreary and cheerless. It didn't appear to have a café or even a shop, as we might have expected to see on a tourist-friendly cycle route. The only bar we saw looked rundown and uninviting. A group of workmen in khaki overalls stood outside the doorway and stared at us suspiciously as we drove slowly by. We continued, hoping that the next village would be a bit more tourist-friendly, but each one was the same as the last. None of them seemed to have any centre or focal point, such as a church or school. The buildings lacked colour, and most houses had the same dull grey concrete facades.

'I don't think it's going to be a very inspiring ride if this is supposed to be one of Slovakia's best cycling routes,' Justi commented, echoing the same thoughts I was having.

'There's a large town coming up. Maybe we'll at least be able to get a snack there?' I suggested with little confidence.

As we neared the town, we noticed signs for hotels and cafés as well as the usual billboard promotions that line the approach roads of most towns in urban Europe.

'What a difference compared to the villages,' Justi commented as we parked close to a tourist information office in what looked like a typically busy, modern European town. With many snack bars, a variety of small shops and two supermarkets, the town was an unlikely contrast to the dreary provincial outlands we'd just driven through. It appeared that the money spent on Slovakia's infrastructure had been heavily weighted towards the major towns and cities.

After a look around the centre, we decided our best option would be to book into a cheap hotel or pension and then cycle an out-and-back route. At least this meant that we wouldn't have to struggle to find a room on the rural back roads. Just on the edge of town, we found a small pension surrounded by a well-tended garden of flowers and shrubs. A blackboard stood propped against the wall outside announcing the room prices, which were extremely modest and well within our meagre budget.

As it was early in the day, and having seen only a handful of other tourists in the town, we were surprised to see that the pension had a manned reception desk. The foyer was bright and modern, and natural light flooded in from the roof skylights above the desk, enhancing the tasteful decoration. The young man on duty spoke fluent English and showed us to a room which, like the foyer, was bright and elegantly understated. We happily agreed to take the place and explained our cycling plans. He seemed mystified that we wanted to ride through the countryside and was even more puzzled when we showed him our cycle-friendly Slovakian maps.

'There aren't any proper cycle routes on these roads,' he said, frowning while pointing at the little blue bike legends marked across the map, 'but there's a cycle path alongside the Danube.'

'OK, thanks for the information. Now that we're here, we'll go for a ride anyway,' I said, knowing that we both wanted a bit of exercise and didn't wish to sit in the car for another day.

'When you come back, bring your bikes in. It's not safe to leave them outside,' he added in a serious tone, just as the hostel warden had done. We wondered how much of an issue theft was in Slovakia as neither of us had noticed any criminal activity or felt a need to be overly wary.

After a quick lunch, we rode out into the countryside and soon arrived at a village. I say 'village' in the broadest sense as, like the others, it didn't appear to have any centre, just a few small detached grey houses equally spaced along the roadside. The next village was the same, so I stopped and leaned my bike against a telegraph pole to check the map, wondering if there was anything interesting we could go and look at. As Justi joined me, a high-pitched screeching sound like feedback at a rock concert made us jump.

A speaker attached to the pole a metre above our heads crackled into life. A man's voice started to make announcements, punctuated with people's names as though he was reading a list of eulogies. A mournful orchestral piece followed. As we left, the dismal tune followed us along the street via the speakers, which were linked to every pole.

'What the heck was that all about?' Justi asked as we left the village and the dreary tones of Radio Cheerless receded in the distance.

When I mentioned it to a Slovene friend on our return, he commented, 'Oh, that'll be the people's radio.'

'The people's radio?'

'Yes, I think the Slovaks just use it for public announcements these days, such as births, deaths, marriages and so on, but in the past, it was used more for government and local council statements.'

To us, it seemed an odd concept that, even in 2005, a villager had to listen to a compulsory radio if they lived out in the sticks in Slovakia. But maybe it was a welcome and comforting thing for many who had grown up with it.

These minor country roads were rougher than we were used to in Slovenia, and we had to concentrate on avoiding the potholes. Occasionally, we'd reach a junction and cross wide roads, still without much traffic, that seemed to be constructed from large concrete rectangular slabs. These roads reminded me of the type I'd seen in military bases, and I imagined their purpose might have been to move military equipment about rapidly when the country had been a satellite of Soviet communism.

At one junction, we watched an elderly lady walking along one of these wide roads, pushing a big-wheeled handcart. She was wearing a headscarf and printed dress and reminded me of the old ladies who worked the fields in Slovenia. The cart was piled high with bags, while pots and pans jangled noisily, attached to the sides by pieces of string. A small white terrier trotted busily alongside, darting between her feet and the wheels. We smiled and said hello but she just stared straight ahead as though locked in her own reality, muttering incoherently as she passed. Unable to find a café or anything of intrigue, we turned around and headed back to our pension.

The next day, we drove south, having decided to ride a section of the cycle path along the Danube. We found another lovely pension just on the edge of a large town called Komárno and booked in for two nights. Once again, we were told earnestly by the receptionist to 'bring your bikes inside. It's not safe.'

The town was placed centrally between Bratislava and Vác, a town in Hungary where the Danube turns sharply south. For this reason, we planned to cycle west towards Bratislava, out and back along the Danube cycle path. The next day, we would cycle east, out and back towards Štúrovo. We rode into the attractive old town centre of Komárno with its beautifully restored medieval buildings and sat for a few moments on the wall of a fountain. The whole town was once under the authority of Hungary and straddled both sides of the Danube, but after the demise of the Austro-Hungarian Empire, it was split into two. The Hungarians got the smaller part, known as Komárom, but even today, the population of Slovakian Komárno is still mostly of Hungarian origin.

We noticed many folk left their bikes unlocked, leaning against the benches and lamp-posts in the square, and wondered again why all our hosts seemed so sure our bikes would be whisked away. I'm sure bike theft exists in Slovakia, as it does in all European countries, but the local cyclists didn't seem unduly worried.

As we left on our ride, we soon discovered that the Slovakian section of the Danube cycle path wasn't as developed as we'd been led to believe. The signed track we started out on soon disappeared into a field. Backtracking, we realised that, to stay closer to the river, we needed to heave our bikes on our shoulders and scale a fence atop one of the levees before we could continue. And so the day continued, with limited signs, difficult access and nowhere to get drinks or refreshments. This was in sharp contrast to Slovenia where every village has at least one bar and a *gostilna* where locals meet to enjoy a drink and chat. The Slovakian section of the Danube cycle path was obviously still in its infancy when we visited. The fact that the tourist board were pushing the country as a great cycling destination seemed premature and was frustrating. The countryside was undoubtedly beautiful, and it wasn't difficult to see the potential for cycle touring if the paths and roads marked on their maps as bike-friendly existed. After a similar experience the following day, we decided to give up on our tour of Slovakia.

To salvage our short holiday, we drove over the border into Hungary and on to Budapest. The buzz and energy of Hungary's capital city were in sharp contrast to the quiet provincial backwaters of Slovakia that we'd just left. The city was hosting an exhibition stage of an international car rally, and we were amazed to see fully tricked-out cars racing around the heavily populated centre. It wasn't long before the sound of the tweaked engines reverberating around the city's tall buildings became tiresome, and we dived into the entrance of an indoor market.

Inside, a beautiful medieval vaulted ceiling spanned the building that was like an Aladdin's cave. With everything from antique Turkish samovars to remote-control model racing cars for sale, it was a veritable emporium to a junk addict like me. Just as I spotted a stall selling old cameras, Justi wisely pulled me away and suggested that we went sightseeing instead as our holiday was almost over. We gave ourselves an hour and took a tram along the river then walked over the famous chain bridge to view the city's incredible waterfront buildings in the hazy afternoon sunshine.

Later that day, we drove home to our apartment in furthest west

Slovenia in just under seven hours—less time than it used to take us to drive from the Scottish Highlands to Liverpool to visit family and friends.

Chapter 23 A Seaside Holiday?

After all our work on the guidebook, which meant spending a lot of time walking in the mountains and hills, Justi suggested we should have a change of scene during the school summer break.

'A seaside holiday. Let's go to the coast,' she said. 'We could go for three weeks, and we'll camp every night to keep the costs down.'

Although I love to visit the coast, I have to admit to not being much of a 'lie on the beach all day' devotee, but I know Justi isn't either.

'What d'you have in mind?' I asked her.

'Montenegro. I've been reading about it—fabulous beaches, the Bay of Kotor and that little island just off the coast where all the rich and famous like Richard Burton and Sophia Loren used to go on their holidays. It sounds idyllic, and I'm sure we'll be able to find a quiet place to camp. You'll get some great photos, and we could go swimming and snorkelling. We could take our bikes too,' she added, trying to hook me with her persuasive enthusiasm and knowing full well my obsessive attitude where cameras and bikes are involved.

I agreed that it would be an interesting change of scene. Who wouldn't? At the same time, I wondered if I'd even be allowed near the beaches of the rich and famous. That evening, I dug out my mildew-riddled Speedos and, after blowing cobwebs and various dead insects out of my snorkel, declared myself ready for our seaside adventure. Lanos would have loved this, but we'd since traded him in for a practical and staid-looking dark blue Volkswagen Polo estate from the same Citroën dealers. We'd left Lanos on the dealer's forecourt looking hopeful that his next owners might be beach lovers, or at least have a garage to protect his shiny metallic jacket from the winter snows.

Leaving the lush Slovenian countryside and the sound of crickets behind, we exchanged euros for kunas at the Croatian border and drove down the coastline to the sound of the much louder cicadas.

We passed the towns of Zadar and Šibenik with their ancient domed cathedrals and churches. Islands shimmered in the heat like parched mosaics floating in the iridescent turquoise waters of the Adriatic Sea, while inland, the pale Dinaric mountains rose above the dry cinnamon-coloured foothills.

As the car didn't have any air conditioning, we drove with the windows open, which meant we reduced our speed. It was early evening by the time we pulled into a campsite near Trogir, a seaside resort located about halfway along the Croatian coastline.

'Phew, I'm baking hot, and it's 10 p.m.,' Justi commented as we lay down in the tent on our inflatable mattress for the night without the need for sleeping bags.

We woke early the next morning and were soon driven from the tent by the rapidly rising temperature and the din of the cicadas.

'I hope we'll find a shadier place to camp tonight,' Justi said as I fried eggs on our single-burner camping stove. I could have cooked them on the bare rock and saved some gas.

It was another long hot day of driving, but we were excited to see Dubrovnik, the most famous Dalmatian town that's usually marketed using Lord Byron's famous quote as being the pearl of the Adriatic.

The coast road was slow and busy, and as we finally approached the exit for Dubrovnik and saw the streams of cars trying to enter and leave the town, we had second thoughts.

'Maybe we could stop on our way back from Montenegro?' I suggested.

'In another three weeks, it will be even busier, but I don't want to face all those crowds today either,' Justi agreed.

We decided to carry on past and were glad about our decision when we stopped by the roadside on a hill. Looking down on the stunningly beautiful red-roofed old town, it looked besieged. The approach road appeared to be gridlocked, and passenger boats were lined up in its medieval harbour; a tourist tragedy that would probably get worse. In another 40 kilometres, with excitement and anticipation, we reached the Montenegrin border. It's strange how we expect a border to mark a distinct change in the land and people. It probably does in many cases, but the only difference we noticed here was the swathe of tall cypress trees that covered the hillside above the Montenegrin border station.

We'd seen cypress trees in Croatia, but they were always in a neat row, usually marking the line of a driveway or church boundary and sometimes planted neatly around the edge of a garden. The Montenegrin cypresses grew randomly, like a wild forest. Otherwise, the land appeared the same, and the cicadas continued their deafening song.

Montenegro wasn't a member of the EU, but it had adopted the euro as its currency in 2002, so we didn't need to change money at the border. Our planned stop for the evening, and, hopefully, the following week, was the famed seaside town of Budva. We took a small ferry to cross the Bay of Kotor to avoid the long drive around its fjord-like waters; something we planned to do on our return journey. The bay is dotted with medieval villages that we hoped to visit, and we'd noticed a campsite on our map.

As we neared Budva, the traffic increased, and we were troubled to see an unexpectedly large number of tourists milling about outside bars and cafés. The crowds became bigger as we drove along Budva's seafront, and it was a moment or two before we realised that many were wearing T-shirts and hats emblazoned with the same motif. I recognised the salacious red lips and tongue of the Rolling Stones logo just before we saw the huge billboard announcing a concert. The old men of rock were coming to town the following day, and the gig was to be held on one of Budva's famous beaches.

Our quiet seaside recess wasn't off to a good start, perhaps worse for Justi. I must confess to quite liking the Stones and had seen them live on a couple of occasions in the '80s, but even so, it was pretty inconvenient of them to disrupt our peaceful holiday. There was only one campsite left without a 'No vacancies' notice. After assuring the stressed-out receptionist that we only had a coffin-sized tent, she showed us a scrubby patch of dead grass between the other tents.

Our neighbours on one side, a couple from Holland, were playing CDs of rock and blues music, while our other neighbour, a middle-aged Serbian Keith Richards wannabe, strummed his guitar, badly, trying to follow the tunes. We noticed most of the campers seemed to be of the happy variety. They were also very relaxed despite the overcrowded conditions. Their laid-back, and in some cases almost horizontal attitude, may have had something to do with the heavy, pungent odour of marijuana that drifted across the campsite.

We knew that Budva and the surrounding coastline would only get busier for the concert, so that evening we decided we would drive inland the next day. Although we were supposed to be having a seaside holiday and a change of scene from the Alps, we were also curious about Montenegro's mountainous Durmitor National Park, which Justi had read about in her research. The park was located in the north of the country, so it was going to involve another few hours in the car, but we wanted to escape the crowds.

The next morning, while I packed the tent away, Justi went to pay for our single night's stay at reception. When she returned, it was apparent things hadn't gone very well.

'Let's get out of here,' she hissed. 'Budva's cashing in on its music venue status.'

'What d'you mean?' I asked.

'We were charged more than twice what the campsite notice board declared because of the "special" circumstances the concert has created.'

We drove out of town, stopping to take photos of Sveti Stefan, the stunningly beautiful islet with its red roofs and honey-coloured stone buildings, the bolthole for the rich and famous who came to stay on this private island paradise and dip their toes in the Adriatic. I wondered if their view of Budva was as good.

We turned away from the Montenegrin coast, and immediately the road began to climb steeply into the hinterland. We only had our old small-scale European road atlas for guidance as we hadn't expected to deviate far from the coast road and our tranquil seaside holiday dream. As we rounded a hairpin bend, we saw the decaying body of a large wolf lying on the verge. Whether it was a road-kill accident or it had been shot, we couldn't find out as the steep incline on the bend wasn't a safe place to stop. We continued to wind our way up the twisting road and eventually reached a vast plateau area that stretched into the distance. The terrain consisted of dry scrub, rocks and small trees—a wild maquis wasteland.

Straight ahead, almost like a mirage shimmering in the heat, we could see what looked like hundreds of cars parked in the maquis. As we drove closer, we could hardly believe our eyes when we saw that our mirage was, in fact, second-hand car dealerships that lined either side of the road. It was bizarre to see hundreds of cars parked up in large gravel forecourts. The whole place seemed to have been hastily constructed and looked completely out of context in the wild surroundings of the high plateau.

'How odd. What on earth d'you think's going on here?' Justi asked as we continued past one car plot after another.

I was none the wiser and wondered why the car dealers would choose to locate themselves in such a remote spot and not prefer to be near the towns on the coast or in the valleys. Later that year, when we were back in the Alps, a Slovenian friend confided that there was a dark side to the Montenegrin 'highland' car salesmen. His (apparently well-known) explanation was that a large number of the cars were stolen from other European countries. He suggested that locals could buy them from the shady dealers at a very low price as long as they would only use them within Montenegro. They would have to pay considerably more if they intended to use them beyond the border as this would involve the purchase of a different set of number plates.

I can't confirm whether there was any truth in my friend's tale, but it was a good story that sounded as colourful and bizarre as the upland auto market looked. As we continued, we noticed that the road signs, especially those indicating smaller settlements, were written in Cyrillic script. Although Cyrillic is one of the most used writing systems in the world, it didn't match our basic road atlas or our even more fundamental knowledge of Montenegro. Looking ahead, we saw a range of limestone mountains bordering the edge of the plateau. Below the mountains sat a large town which, like the car plots, looked strangely misplaced in the wild, rocky landscape. From our viewpoint on the road, it didn't look like an attractive place, but in retrospect, its bleak surroundings perhaps deceived us.

We hadn't planned to visit this part of Montenegro, so we hadn't done our research. The town is called Cetinje, and if we'd known that it's probably Montenegro's most culturally rich and diverse municipality, we would have spent some time there. Instead, we took a higher road into the hills, following signs for the Lovćen National Park.

Eager to stretch our legs, we pulled into a car park and followed a long series of steps that led us to an impressive building perched on a hilltop. The building was the Njegoš mausoleum. Petar II Petrović-Njegoš was a Montenegrin prince-bishop, poet and philosopher who got his wish to be interred at the top of his favourite mountain. Unfortunately, it wasn't to be much of a resting place for him. His body had to make several trips up and down the mountain due to wars and politics, with his final resting place being destroyed, rebuilt and relocated on many occasions. His most recent, and hopefully last, move was in 1974. The view from his chosen mountain was truly spectacular; it was as though the whole of Montenegro lay at our feet, and we stood in awe as a light breeze ruffled through the clumps of ochre grasses and colourful alpine flowers that grew among the rocks. We didn't have long to savour the moment as, realising we still had a lot of driving on minor roads to reach the Durmitor mountains, we quickly retraced our steps back down to the car. As we drove further inland, the road surface became terrible.

'Go right...no, left!' Justi shouted as she tried to warn me about the potholes that littered the road.

It was impossible to dodge all of them, and some could have swallowed a donkey. Several times, the car tilted sharply as we dropped into suspension-wrecking craters. As we manoeuvred slowly between the pits of despair, a large striped hornet settled on the windscreen and looked in at me menacingly. Instinctively, I tried to wind my window up, but I already knew it was too late.

'It's going to come through my window and sting me on the neck,' I declared to Justi as my hand rotated the handle with Superman speed. I had no idea why I declared such a thing, but I felt strangely resigned to my unpleasant premonition. And that's precisely what happened.

'Ow, yer bugger!' I exclaimed as my striped attacker stung me with its red-hot needle before casually flying back out through the window like a military helicopter that had just completed a successful combat mission. I pulled over on the hot and dusty road, and Justi removed the sting from my neck.

Looking at our atlas, which showed Montenegro to be about three centimetres square, we guessed we still had a fair distance to drive on minor roads, and with the day's events so far, we began to wonder whether it was a good holiday destination after all. A motor home approached, the first vehicle we'd seen for almost an hour, and as it passed, the young couple in the cab smiled and waved enthusiastically. They had a Slovene registration and had recognised ours too. Their friendly faces cheered us up a bit, and we continued.

Eventually, with a sigh of relief, we joined a slightly better road that led to the Durmitor National Park and the main town of the area—Žabljak. As the park's mountains came more into view, we could see that they looked similar to the steep limestone peaks of the Slovene Alps, but without as much tree cover. We drove past an open plain near the foot of the hills where wooden A-framed houses stood among clumps of coarse grasses, bringing to mind the similar architecture of a Scandinavian landscape.

Just before we reached Žabljak, we found a nice-looking campsite. The owners, a middle-aged couple, fetched their daughter who could speak English. It was their first season running the campsite, and they nodded their heads and smiled eagerly as their daughter told us we were their first British guests. After setting up camp and restoring our jangled motoring nerves with a pot of tea, we drove into town.

Žabljak was a curious mix of buildings and infrastructure. Houses with wood cladding and colourful metal roofs rubbed shoulders with shops and hotels constructed in 1970s-style concrete communist architecture. As it was only a small town with hardly any traffic, we were surprised to see two uniformed policemen directing the few cars that passed along its main street. We decided that they must have been on training duty as stopping individual vehicles to wave another one on looked comically officious and over the top.

Our first port of call was the tourist information office where we met Tomo, a fountain of local knowledge. He spoke fluent English and was eager to share his language skills with a pair of native speakers. As well as the best places to eat, Tomo told us about the best routes in the mountains and also suggested that we shouldn't leave without seeing the nearby Tara Canyon.

He proudly told us that the Tara was the largest of its kind in Europe and second only to America's Grand Canyon as the deepest river canyon in the world. He also recommended that we should take a short walk to see the Črno Jezero (Black Lake), a famous beauty spot close to the town. Tomo explained that it was just one of a system of lakes in the Durmitor National Park that were linked by a geological network of underground limestone caverns. He showed a deeply passionate knowledge of the Durmitor landscape and told us he'd studied geology as a graduate. After sharing our passion for the peaks of the Julian Alps, we appeared to gain his confidence as fellow admirers of limestone geology. He told us he believed the Durmitor mountain region to be under threat from both his government and Russian property developers.

'Russians are buying land here to build houses, and they're interfering with the geology,' he declared.

We looked at him, slightly puzzled and wondering how a few new houses on the edge of the national park could cause such cataclysmic interference.

'They're dynamiting the rocks and levelling the ground for foundations. It's affecting the water levels, and my government turns a blind eye,' he added sadly.

He went on to explain that, even if the newly built houses were outside the park boundaries, the dynamiting affected water levels within the lakes and catchment areas because of the complex interconnecting geology of limestone.

We thanked him for sharing his knowledge and bought a map of the park. As we left, he called after us, 'And don't forget to see the Black Lake—it mightn't be here for much longer!'

Walking along the high street, we spotted one of the cafés that Tomo had recommended and decided to get some lunch. As we viewed the daily specials menu board, the café owner appeared on the veranda. He was a tall man with a neat moustache and was wearing a crisp white shirt topped with a tweed jacket. He smiled and, half bowing, welcomed us with a sweep of his arm to his eatery.

'It's Basil Fawlty,' I whispered irreverently to Justi as he pulled out chairs for us at a table.

Like John Cleese's well-known TV hotelier character, he pompously recommended we try certain dishes. Suddenly, putting his hand out to excuse himself, he turned aside, clearing his nasal cavities in a loud manner not for the faint-hearted, and spat over the veranda into the undergrowth beside the café. Justi and I exchanged shocked glances, but despite this, his friendly oddball character had us already forgiving him for his heinous nasal crime. However, a young French couple sitting at the next table were finding the Slavic Basil Fawlty's behaviour somewhat harder to bear.

'*C'est déplorable!*' said the young man to no one in particular while his pretty girlfriend put her hand to her mouth in shock.

The maître d' continued, seemingly unaware that his noisome

throaty discord might be deemed offensive or inappropriate, and stood attentively poised with pencil and notebook to take our order. With a smile and a polite bow, he turned on his heel towards the kitchen only to hesitate just before the door to clear the contents of his cavities once again into the shrubbery.

'*C'est dégoûtant*! (It's disgusting!)' cried the young Frenchman as I wondered where we'd get smelling salts for his distraught partner who looked about to faint.

Despite the maître d's dubious behaviour, our lunch was excellent. Some of the dishes on the menu such as *pljeskavica* (a spiced meat burger) and *čevapčiči* (grilled skinless sausages), we recognised from Slovenia, but we discovered that their origins were, in fact, more Montenegrin and Serbian. Other dishes included *sarma* (vine leaves stuffed with mince and rice), *prebranac* (bean casserole) and *durmitorski skorop* (a local, salty cottage cheese).

As we left the restaurant, the Balkan Basil gave us a cheery wave before expertly aiming another mucous misdemeanour into the pot plants.

Chapter 24 Montenegro—Heights and Depths

The next day, we returned to Žabljak, hoping to hire a tandem bicycle we'd spotted in a sports shop the previous day when the store had been closed for lunch.

'You don't want mountain bikes? We have very good mountain bikes for hire,' said the young man worriedly as though we'd made a terrible decision regarding our choice of transport.

'No, the tandem will be fine, thanks,' I replied.

Although we'd never owned a tandem, we'd borrowed one for a month from a friend while in Scotland and loved it. Apart from it being a lot of fun, we'd found it a great way to ride together, regardless of our different physical abilities and pace. We'd noticed that riding a tandem almost always induces a smile and a cheerful response from people. It also meant we were able to chat easily as we rode along.

We left our details, and I helped the guy wheel our lengthy conveyance out of the shop and stand it against the kerb. Before I had time to check it over with the assistant, he locked the shop and dashed off in a minibus to collect a group of adrenalin addicts who had been rafting in the Tara Canyon. I went on the front as 'pilot', while Justi was the 'stoker' at the rear. We adjusted the seat heights, and after looking over our shoulders, counted to three and pushed off from the kerb. It was in a high gear, so the effort to get moving had us wobbling ungraciously in the gutter as I fumbled to change the shift lever.

'Change gear,' cried Justi as we lumbered forward, just missing a pedestrian who was about to step into the road.

'It won't change. The gears won't change,' I yelled in frustration.

Fortunately, we soon built up a good head of steam that complimented our lung-busting, hernia-inducing high gear. Before long, we were passing the town boundary sign and pedalling our way along the quiet country road.

'I think it'll be best if we stop at the campsite on the way, and I'll see if I can fix the gears,' I suggested.

As we neared the turn, I squeezed the brakes gently, and nothing happened. I squeezed harder; still nothing.

'Slow down; you'll miss our turn!' cried an urgent voice behind me.

By now, my knuckles were white with squeezing the levers, and I'd resorted to using both feet to skim the gravelly gutter to slow us down. Just as I thought my shoes were about to burst into flames, we came to an ungainly stop on the verge, a good ten metres past our turn.

'I think I'd better check the brakes as well,' I said, stating the obvious to my ashen-faced stoker.

While Justi calmed her nerves by making a pot of tea, I gave the tandem a much-needed service. My love of cycling meant I'd acquired enough skills to build up and maintain bikes, so I didn't find it difficult to have the tandem ready to roll safely by the time we'd drunk our tea.

Our route was going to be a long loop through the countryside with its small farmsteads and fields and across an open, heathery plain with the Durmitor mountains as the backdrop. Leaving the campsite, we were soon bowling along rather more safely through the rural landscape. We passed families using pitchforks to stack and gather hay in the fields. The children and teenagers waved to us, smiling enthusiastically, while older family members stood and stared bemused as we pedalled past. We noticed how lofty the older Montenegrin folk looked and weren't surprised when we later discovered them to be one of the tallest ethnic groups in Europe. Younger men and women, in their late 20s and 30s, didn't appear to be as imposing as their parents, and we wondered if the discrepancy was the result of dietary deficiencies induced by the Balkan Wars of the '90s.

With the breeze at our backs, we soon left behind the small rural pastures and found ourselves on a plateau of open moorland.

'Stop!' Justi called as we rounded a bend on a narrow road that wouldn't have looked out of place in the Scottish Highlands.

She'd spotted what looked like a group of ancient standing stones a short distance away. With no signs or information boards evident to suggest a site of interest, we leaned the tandem carefully against a boulder and walked over to investigate. The stones were randomly dotted around an area of about 50 square metres. Some of them leaned at sharp angles, while others had fallen over and lay half-buried in the thick tussocks of grass. All of them were intricately carved with strange symbols and decorations. We had no idea what they were or represented, but their location on the wide-open plateau with the Durmitor mountains as a backdrop made it feel a very special place.

After we arrived back in Žabljak and returned the tandem, we called into the tourist office to see if Tomo could tell us anything about the standing stones.

'They're known as *stećci* stones,' he told us. 'They're quite a mystery. Not much is known about them, but they're not from prehistory. Some historians believe they may be of Greek origin and were supposedly made as tombstones between the 12th and 16th centuries.'

While 40,000 people were scrunched together to see another group of venerable Stones at Budva, we'd enjoyed the *stećci* in peace and isolation.

In the early evening, we set out to find the Tara Canyon, thinking that if Tomo's description concerning its dimensions was correct, it shouldn't be too difficult. With our new, detailed map, we followed the road out of Žabljak before turning onto a lane and past a group of rundown houses. This smaller road was deeply potholed, its surface cracked and broken like Emmental cheese. As we began to wonder if we'd made a wrong turn, we spotted a small hand-painted wooden sign which read 'Tara', hammered to a post. The bent, rusty nails that once held it in place protruded into space, and the sign pointed vaguely skywards. As there was nowhere else to go, we followed the narrow road for another 100 metres to its end at a muddy turning area. Another rough hand-painted sign for the canyon pointed along an overgrown path that led between dense glades of small pine trees and juniper bushes.

'Extraordinary that this path will lead us to one of the world's greatest natural wonders,' said Justi as we fought our way through the undergrowth.

Suddenly, the ground fell away, and we found ourselves staring into an unimaginable abyss. For a moment, we stood silently, unable to grasp the immense depth and size of the canyon. Looking down the 1,300 metres to the bottom, we could just make out the thin strand of white and hear the rushing water of the mighty river in the depths. Red continental pines, like Scots pines, clung with gnarled roots like eagles' claws to the upper walls below the lip of the canyon. We clambered down a little way between rock-filled grooves and chimneys to find a better position to take photos. As we sat on a ledge, silently taking in the view, the sky darkened dramatically, and light rain began to fall. Just as we began to think we'd witnessed the best of the day, the sun burst through the deep indigo-coloured clouds and lit the walls of the canyon with a bright curtain of light that formed rainbows on the glistening rocks. We returned to our tent feeling humbled but elated at having experienced such a wonderful day.

We arose early the next morning and packed a rucksack for a trip to climb one of the Durmitor peaks on the eastern edge of the range. The terrain reminded us of the Julian Alps with its pale limestone rocks and short grass dotted with a colourful variety of pretty alpine flowers. Also familiar was the presence of caves—a typical feature of the karst geology.

We reached the summit around midday, where a group of five or six walkers were relaxing and enjoying the view. A man who appeared about 40 years old introduced himself after he heard us chatting. Branko, who had excellent English, was a teacher from Serbia. He was happy to talk, eager to understand why we'd decided to move to Slovenia and wanted to hear our impressions of Montenegro.

He described to us how the recent Balkan Wars had made life very challenging and that the whole region was still undergoing a period of recovery. He and his wife were finding it difficult to live on the €400 a month salary that he took home. His day in the mountains seemed to be his escape from the stress of everyday life.

'There are wealthy people in my country,' he told us. 'They made a lot of money by selling weapons to the different opposing factions.'

Branko appeared proud and pleased to hear how much we were enjoying our holiday at Durmitor. Checking his watch, he left with a friendly handshake to return to his car in the valley as he still had a 150-kilometre drive to reach his home town in Central Serbia. We stayed on the summit and basked in the sunshine for another hour, feeling thankful and appreciative for our comparatively carefree lives in Slovenia.

Later that day, as we walked along the broad gravel path past the Black Lake on our return to Žabljak, we noticed a man strolling casually towards us. He was about 50 years old, his greying hair greased and brushed back. He was dressed in an expensive-looking black shirt and trousers and wore polished black Cuban-heeled boots. He had heavy gold chains and medallions draped around his neck, and a thick gold bracelet and Rolex watch adorned his wrists. He looked like the stereotypical image of a TV or movie gangster, and I was immediately reminded of Branko's comments about arms dealers.

'Good afternoon,' he said as we met on the track.

'Er, hello,' we managed weakly, both feeling suspicious and unsure of this unlikely-looking character.

'I hope you've had a good walk?' he enquired in a cultured English accent. 'Please allow me to introduce myself. I'm Zoran. I heard you chatting, so I know that you are English.' Zoran went on to explain he owned a holiday home near Žabljak and was out for his favourite evening stroll at the Black Lake. He was the epitome of charm and almost managed to dispel the feelings of menace we'd felt, or imagined. He told us he'd learned English when he'd spent a few years living in London.

Despite his friendly manner, we thought it perhaps best not to ask him what he did for a living.

We spent the next few days exploring the national park and drove down the steep, winding road to see the Đurđevića Tara Bridge that crosses the river. A single motorcycle was parked near the end of the bridge when we arrived. The 365-metre span of the arched structure is a jaw-droppingly impressive sight, and we walked out to the middle to peer over the balustrade at the powerful river over 170 metres below. Tomo had told us that the bridge was the longest and tallest of its kind in Europe when completed in 1940, and to us, it was another amazingly well-kept secret of Montenegro. We didn't see anyone canoeing the river that day, and apart from the German motorcycling couple also enjoying the views, we didn't meet any other tourists.

Fast forward ten years and, apparently, the Tara River sees hundreds of canoeists and rafters each day in the summer months, and the canyon and bridge are home to an extreme zip line and buttock-clenching bungee jump.

By the end of the week, we'd come up with a vague rescue plan for our seaside holiday.

Chapter 25 Out of This World

Another camper had told us about a beautiful beach located further east along the Montenegrin coast, describing it as the nicest in Montenegro. We planned to drive south-west to the coast past Lake Skadar which formed part of the natural border with Albania. We also hoped to visit a famous monastery on the way that had a spectacular location, built into a high cliff face.

Before we left, I hoped to climb the highest peak of the Durmitor mountains—Bobotov Kuk. I expected this to involve a bit of persuasion on my part as Justi seemed very keen to substitute beaches for mountains and her swimsuit for fleeces. After adding a little more wine than usual to one of my one-pan camp casseroles, I prepared to make my move. Justi, though, beat me to it.

'D'you mind if we stay here one more day?' she asked. 'I'd quite like to have a restful day tomorrow. Why d'you look so surprised? We can move on if you really don't want to stay.'

'Er, no, no, I don't mind. I mean, it's supposed to be a holiday after all, isn't it? I'll go and do a hill while you enjoy a relaxing day.'

I probably didn't sound very convincing, and a twinkle in Justi's eye made me suspect she'd already anticipated my wish for another day in the hills. Bless her little cotton hiking socks.

Early the next morning, Justi gave me a lift into Žabljak and dropped me off at the start of my walk. Feeling invigorated by the cool morning air, I was eager to be on my way, while Justi looked equally keen to be heading back to the tent and her book.

The Black Lake lived up to its name; like the surrounding forest, its waters were dark while the early morning sun lit the high summits beyond with a warming orange light. Above the lake, I passed a group of wooden animal shelters with shingle roofs in a small grassy ravine. A lone shepherd was busy repairing a fence while hundreds of long-eared sheep milled about him, bleating loudly. A little further on, I passed another two huts with red metal roofs. These were bivouac shelters for walkers and climbers to use.

Around the huts, an unofficial campsite had sprung up, and five or six brightly coloured tents were pitched on the idyllic alp. A young couple sat outside one of the tents, sipping coffee from steaming mugs, and nodded indifferently, looking not yet fully awake. After about three hours, I reached a high saddle above a wild, boulder-filled corrie where the path steepened considerably to ascend the final ridge that led to the summit. About 200 metres ahead, I saw another hiker making his way up the airy path. As I was feeling very fit and fresh, I made it my aim to try and catch up with the lone hiker. Try as I might, I hardly gained any ground, and he reached the top before me.

Being the highest peak of the range, the views from Bobotov Kuk were incredible. Long ridges serrated with rocky pinnacles gave way to grassy alps and forested valleys. I could now see more of the Durmitor lakes, cupped like precious sapphires in the wild corries and grassy hollows.

The lean and fit hiker who had kept up a blistering pace ahead of me turned out to be from Scotland. Andrew, who was about 30 years old, had arrived in Žabljak the previous day, having spent over a month wandering the mountains and valleys of Albania and Kosovo. He'd had quite an adventure, and he told me he was treated with deep suspicion when entering villages in Kosovo and sometimes feared for his safety. But on the whole, he received kind treatment from the locals when they discovered he was Scottish. The people of Kosovo had endured some of the worst atrocities of the Balkan Wars. While much of the region had begun to recover and rebuild, Kosovo continued to experience instances of violent unrest.

Andrew was intrigued to hear that I'd lived in his home country, and it seemed surreal to be chatting about familiar places and hills in the Highlands while eating our sandwiches on the summit of a mountain in Montenegro. We parted company back at the saddle as Andrew was trekking west across the mountains with another two weeks left of his holiday. As I made my way back down the path, I passed groups of walkers on their way up and was pleased I'd made an early start and only shared the summit with the quiet, adventurous Highlander. As I neared the half dozen tents above the lake, I was surprised but delighted to see Justi walking towards me. She'd enjoyed a peaceful, relaxing day at the campsite but was now happy to stretch her legs.

'As it's our last evening here, let's go out for dinner. Tomo told me about a fantastic restaurant,' she enthused.

And so we did. For the price of a UK takeaway, we tucked into a fabulous, three-course dinner with a bottle of local wine. We'd enjoyed our visit to Montenegro's mountains, but the lack of infrastructure in and around the Durmitor National Park had surprised us. It seemed odd that the Tara Canyon, like the historic *stećci* tombstones, wasn't being promoted with the usual tourist trappings such as visitor centres, information boards and parking areas that you would see in other parts of Europe. On the other hand, we'd enjoyed the peace and sense of seeing a place as the locals themselves experience it.

We left Žabljak and headed south, back towards the coast, passing a large town called Nikšić, which, like Cetinje, looked strangely out of place located amid the rocky maquis-covered landscape.

'We'll be turning off soon for the monastery,' said Justi as she carefully scrutinised our tatty road atlas.

A sign for Ostrog Monastery confirmed the way, and as we swung left from the main road, we got a glimpse of our destination. High up on the side of a long mountain range, we could see what looked like a white church built into the vertical cliff face.

'Wow! It looks amazing, but bloody hell, look at the road.'

Justi's apprehension was justified, and I found myself gripping the steering wheel more tightly as we started up the startlingly steep and narrow road. Without any crash barriers, and with just the occasional row of small edging stones, the enormous vertical drops had me concentrating hard as I negotiated each hairpin bend, hoping we wouldn't meet another vehicle. We both fell silent, and I even considered muttering a prayer to Saint Basil of Ostrog whose remains lie in the monastery.

With a mutual sigh of relief, we finally reached a small car park and turning point below the impressive edifice. A long row of market stalls sold a variety of religious paraphernalia, but among the plastic saints and model churches, we recognised the face of Radovan Karadžić, an infamous politician, printed on T-shirts, scarves and tea towels. At the time, he was on the run having been indicted for war crimes, but it seemed he was still a popular character within Montenegro and Serbia.

We decided not to go into the monastery building but chose to sit and admire the view across the Montenegrin plains from its airy location. After an equally hair-raising descent, we continued towards the coast past Lake Skadar, the biggest freshwater lake in Southern Europe.

We stopped to take photos near the shore and watched the small fishing boats bobbing on the choppy surface until they disappeared from view in the vast expanse of the lake. We were intrigued by the rugged mountains of Albania towering above the shimmering waters to the east.

Leaving the lake behind, we took a narrow winding road that led towards the coast and, hopefully, the beach. We found a small campsite that looked like it had once been a productive olive grove. We pitched our tent between two ancient olive trees with twisted, gnarly branches and a canopy of dense, silvery leaves, and went off in search of our idyllic beach.

When we arrived at the waterfront, we were disappointed to find that the shoreline consisted of large pebbles and stones rather than the soft golden sand we'd imagined. We were even more disconcerted to see large amounts of litter. Hundreds of people lay sunbathing on thick camping mats, while empty bottles and tins lay randomly strewn around them on the rocky beach.

With our relaxing seaside holiday proving elusive, the next morning we drove along the coast past Budva to the Bay of Kotor and followed the road inland around the fjord. Our disappointment over not yet having found our dream beach was soon forgotten as we enjoyed the atmosphere and sights of the ancient towns around the bay—Kotor with its historic Venetian fortifications, and Risan with the remains of an Illyrian acropolis on its hillside. That evening, we pitched our tent on a small campsite near an inlet in the bay and enjoyed a magnificent sunset. While the sound of the cicadas gradually died away, we sat sipping beers on a rickety wooden jetty and watched the warm orange glow on the mountain summits fade to hues of dark blue and purple.

While I'd been cooking dinner, Justi had been scouring the map, still hoping to find an ideal seaside location.

'I think we just need to head towards home, and maybe we'll find somewhere nice on the way back,' she said. 'Trouble is, the map can't show us how busy it's likely to be,' she added wistfully.

Despite not fulfilling our seaside holiday dream, we'd enjoyed our time in Montenegro more than we could have imagined. The Durmitor mountains, the Tara Canyon, the local people and delicious food were all treasures that seemed little known in Europe at the time. The next day, we drove back over the border and retraced our outward journey along the Dalmatian coast. Even though it was only ten days since we'd driven this way, the traffic had become heavier as the busiest weeks of the season approached.

We passed Dubrovnik, still not wishing to battle our way through its visiting crowds. Around lunchtime, we turned off the main drag and followed a quieter road that led to a long peninsula called Pelješac that Justi had noticed on our map. We passed by an ancient town protected by a huge medieval stone wall that continued through the steep hills beyond. Compared to the mainland coastline, the peninsula was relatively free from the hustle and bustle of tourism.

After passing many small vineyards neatly arranged on rocky terraces, we arrived at a pretty little fishing village where we spotted a hand-painted sign for a campsite and turned off onto a very rough gravel track. This led us to a tiny ramshackle campsite where a few tents and hammocks took up the available space between the stands of sweet-smelling pine trees. Apart from a short row of brick-built toilets, and showers without doors, there were no other buildings. Near the showers, the campsite prices were displayed on a chalkboard beside a rusty fridge that thrummed loudly. Even taking into account the basic facilities, it was very cheap.

'Excuse me, can you tell us where the reception is, please?' we asked a very relaxed-looking Dutchman swinging nonchalantly in a hammock.

'There isn't any reception. Just make your camp. Stejpan will come in the evening, or maybe the morning, and you will pay him,' he informed us in a no-stress-here, carefree manner.

After pitching the tent, we walked the short distance to where we could hear the gentle lapping of the warm Adriatic Sea on the rocky shore. Emerging from the pine trees, we stepped onto a beach where the tranquil waves swished and hissed meditatively as they caressed the pebbles. No more than a dozen people were either lazing on the shore or swimming in the beautiful sparkling waters of the small bay.

'This looks more like it,' Justi said excitedly. 'Let's go a bit further and see what's around the corner of the bay.'

We walked along the beach and soon found ourselves clambering over steep rocks on the little headland. Eventually, we came to a narrow ledge that cut horizontally across a vertical wall about fifteen metres above the water before disappearing around a corner. Enjoying the challenge of a scramble on the warm, rough rock, we made our way along the ledge to see what lay around the corner. An easy path through a jumble of boulders led down to a small cove in an out-of-this-world, isolated setting.

'This is it; this is the place we've been looking for,' Justi remarked happily as we spread our picnic blanket on a honey-coloured slab of rock. From then on, each day we packed snorkels, fins and towels into a rucksack and made our way carefully along the rocks to our secret, idyllic cove. Most mornings, when Stejpan arrived in his old battered van to collect camp fees, he brought freshly caught fish that we'd buy for our lunch and cook at our cove.

It was a difficult place to leave and remains in our memories as the best seaside holiday we've ever had.

Chapter 26 Should We Stay, or Should We Go?

During the May bank holiday, Justi and I managed to book cheap flights to the UK to visit our families. We also took a few days out to visit friends and walk in the hills of North Wales. We both felt a deep sense of familiarity as we walked along the river at Betws-y-Coed, where bunches of late daffodils stood between the gnarled roots of oak trees with their canopy of fresh new leaves. This familiarity was combined with an equally deep feeling of contentment as we walked past the sparkling waters of Llyn Crafnant in the bright sunshine and up onto the hills. The almond-coconut fragrance of gorse and the pungent scent of the emerging bracken flooded our senses and brought back a thousand memories of our days spent in the British hills.

I was starting to feel a little homesick, and I suspected that Justi's contemplative silence meant that she was feeling the same. Then it happened; it had to happen. A small lamb, startled by our presence, jumped up out of the heather a few metres ahead of us and bleated pathetically for its mum as it stumbled through the thick growth on its tiny spindly limbs.

'Aww, look at the little one,' squealed Justi in an equally pathetic and endearing manner. I had to agree; it was an incredible sight, and I knew it would make Justi air her contemplative thoughts with me.

'D'you think we should come back to the UK?' she asked.

It was a difficult question to answer. Although I too was having similar longings to return, I knew that we both felt we had a lot more opportunities and discoveries to make in Slovenia.

'It's the not knowing. We can never put roots down and make plans while just having a yearly contract,' she explained.

'I know what you mean,' I agreed. 'Let's see how we feel once we're back in Slovenia,' I suggested, unable to offer anything more useful at that moment.

Back at Cath and Vic's in Southport, we discovered a parcel had arrived for us from Jonathan, our publisher. It contained several copies of our newly published guidebook to the Julian Alps. It was a deeply satisfying moment to see finally the fruits of our labours in print, and we celebrated the moment with Cath and Vic generously supplying lunch and a nice bottle of wine.

It was also a huge relief after weeks of editing tweaks and re-checking small changes to some of the routes. It's a simple fact that a guidebook can be out of date before it's even published due to the ever-developing tourist infrastructure in mountainous regions. New roads are made, and old landmarks such as restaurants and hotels can close overnight or new ones spring up within weeks. Even sections of the trails in the mountains can sometimes change. The Julian Alps are prone to sizeable rockfalls caused by minor earthquakes or heavy rainfall and the relatively young geological age of the range.

Once we were back in Slovenia, I resumed my role, which was still mainly as a house husband. Working on the guidebook had given me a much-needed sense of purpose and meant that I'd spent more time away from our apartment. I started to think about the possibility of writing another book, this time about a long-distance trail that started in the far east of the country and crossed all the mountainous regions of Slovenia to finish at the coast. I would need to wait, though, before mentioning it to Justi as she was still troubled about taking on yet another yearly contract in the primary school.

I continued to send my photographs off to picture libraries and received a small irregular income in return that helped towards the bills. A friend who came out for a walking holiday had passed on my contact details to a couple of Brits he'd chanced to meet on his inbound flight. They'd told him they'd just bought some properties near Lake Bled and were in the process of converting them into holiday homes. My pal had suggested I might be available to help and, hearing that I lived locally, the Brits were keen to contact me. This resulted in some work for me and, although sporadic, it helped as a buffer when we found ourselves with unexpected large bills such as repairs for the car. The work involved painting, decorating, trips to IKEA to collect and build pieces of furniture, gardening and other odd jobs.

It was about this time that a Slovene friend, Bine, the husband of a teacher colleague of Justi's, persuaded me to join the local camera club. I enjoyed meeting the club members, and their photographs inspired me, but the technical discussions about digital imaging were well beyond my rudimentary Slovene language skills, and I soon began to lose interest. Bine recognised and understood my dilemma and tried his best to help by kindly offering to translate. However, despite his much-appreciated efforts, his English was relatively basic, and the situation remained unresolved as we both struggled to understand the difficult topics of digital photo programmes. He never gave up, though, with his generous help and encouragement, and suggested that, with his assistance, I should arrange an exhibition of my photos.

I accepted his kind offer, and within a week, he'd helped me select a suitable bunch of pictures that would be displayed in the entrance to the theatre and library in Jesenice. I was a little surprised when he told me that the exhibition would start at a specific time, 6:30 p.m., on the Friday and that I should meet him there. I was surprised because I'd imagined that my photos would be informally hung on the walls of the entrance hallway, courtesy of the caretaker, and that I had no reason to be there. I thought it was probably just an opportunity to have a beer and catch up with Bine.

On the Friday, I was working in Bled for the Brits who owned the holiday homes. At around 6 p.m., I finished the last bit of painting and, still wearing my paint-splattered overalls, jumped in the car to drive to Jesenice, eager to see how my pictures looked, hanging in a public place. I'd somehow managed to daub an annoying amount of white gloss paint into my hair, and it had become caked on my hands and the car's steering wheel.

As I entered the building, I was shocked to see a sizeable crowd of smartly dressed folk milling about in the foyer, sipping wine and selecting canapés from carefully laid-out trays. Bine appeared in a shirt and tie and shook my tacky hand then immediately introduced me to a tall man wearing an elegant suit. He was the mayor, and my shock turned to acute embarrassment as I tried in vain to wipe my paint-covered hands quickly on my dirty overalls before shaking his hand.

'Er...please forgive my appearance. I've just come from work you see an—'

'Don't worry. It's not a problem,' said the mayor, and I believed he meant it.

He spoke kindly as he asked me why Justi and I had chosen Slovenia as a place to live. After a brief chat, I made my excuses and headed off to the loo where I quickly discarded my overalls, though the old working jeans and ragged T-shirt I had on underneath were only marginally more acceptable.

Back in the foyer, someone coughed to get everyone's attention, and a member of the photography club introduced a group of children wearing traditional Slovene costumes. They were from one of the local music schools, and the room hushed as they began to play and sing folk songs in note-perfect harmony. A speech from one of the club members followed the music, and then I was asked to step forward to receive a certificate accompanied by polite applause.

I tried my best to stand tall and willed myself to look smart as I accepted my certificate, but I knew I looked a mess. I slunk back into the shadows of the foyer, trying to make myself as inconspicuous as possible, but a young lady accosted me holding a microphone and accompanied by her burly colleague carrying a suspiciously large video camera on his shoulder.

'Hi, I'm Urška from Slovenia TV. Can we do a short interview, please?'

The lesson I learned that evening was how formal and organised the Slovene people can be and how they make even the smallest local events and happenings into something memorable and special. There's quite extraordinary support for any kind of cultural event, though they're equally forgiving of foreigners who don't understand their customs and traditions. The Slovenes are also wonderfully honest, however, and, like the language, can be very direct, which is something British folk can find difficult. As people indulged in the food and wine again, a man approached me after studying my photos.

'I think maybe two of your images are OK. The others are not so good,' he said, before nodding politely and making for the door.

'Thanks,' I called after him, thinking, *Well…two out of twenty-five is surely better than none.*

A few more people came to tell me what they thought of my photos, and thankfully, on the whole, they were more appreciative.

If you're ever invited to a Slovene public event, big or small, expect lengthy speeches, an orderly formality and lots of delicious homemade food and wine.

*****

Justi's first year as a primary school assistant in Jesenice had been good. Polona ran a tight ship, and the working atmosphere and relationship between the staff were both productive and positive. This scenario was echoed too by the children who seemed both happy and confident. On the whole, Justi enjoyed teaching the kids, who in Slovene primary schools are aged between six and fourteen, but by the end of the school year, she felt that she needed something a bit more challenging to stretch her professional skills.

Polona had assured her that her contract would be renewed should she wish to stay.

'What would you like to do then? Are we staying, or are we going back to the UK?' I asked, knowing that her malcontent would grow like a cancer if it wasn't checked.

'I really don't want to go back to the UK. It's so beautiful here, but I know I'll need to do something else, something more,' she replied.

I could hear the frustration and sadness in her voice and wondered how on earth the situation could be resolved as the contract would have to be signed by the end of the week. Although there had been moments when we'd both felt homesick for our families and friends, I didn't want to leave yet. Exploring the Julian Alps for the guidebook had infused me with a passion to experience more of the great outdoor scene Slovenia had to offer. Cycling the quiet roads and swimming in crystal-clear lakes during the hot summer months, coupled with skiing and snowshoeing in the winter, why would we want to leave?

Even on our meagre earnings, we were still easily able to budget for enjoyable coffee and cake treats in Slovenia's reasonably priced bars and cafés.

The day before Justi was due to sign her contract with the primary school, she returned home from work with her face lit by a beaming smile.

'I've got some great news!' she exclaimed. 'I've been offered work in the grammar school, and it comes with a four-year contract!'

'Wow! How did that happen?'

'A colleague told me that the grammar school was asking for native speaker language teachers for a European scheme linked to the one I'm already working for. After making enquiries at the grammar school—'

'The one next door to the primary school?' I interrupted.

'Yes, right there,' she said. 'So, after asking during my break, I was offered a post in the new European Classes Scheme. The principal explained that, although it would be part-time in the first year, it will become full-time next year.'

'Would that give you the challenge you're looking for, d'you think?'

'Yes, definitely. But the part-time commitment in the first year will make it impossible to carry on at the primary school, so I'd lose too much salary.'

'Hmm, is there any way around it, d'you think?'

'I'll speak to Palona and see what she says. It's too good an opportunity not to try and make it work.'

She needn't have worried, as when she explained the situation to Polona, she offered her a contract for a year's part-time work. The incentive to work at the grammar school was strong; she would be a teacher in her own right, not just an assistant. The students were aged fifteen to nineteen, bright young adults eager to learn.

'This is hilarious. I'll be called a professor if I teach at the grammar school,' Justi enthused.

In the British system, a professor is an academic who has reached the top rungs of a university career, while in Slovenia, all secondary school teachers are known as professors. It seemed that, once again, we'd been offered an opportunity to seize the day. So we did.

Opening two ice-cold beers, we sat outside under the tree that shaded Bryn's grave from the bright warm sunshine that beamed from the impossibly blue Slovene skies.

'When we first came to Slovenia, I only ever imagined we'd be here for one school year,' Justi commented, 'and now we seem to be making a life here.'

She was right, and we'd managed to accomplish it all on a shoestring budget. We raised our glasses and made a toast to living on the Sunny Side of the Julian Alps. At least for another four years…

Our story continues in *The Sunny Side of the Alps: A B&B in Slovenia*.

Message from the Author

I sincerely thank you for reading this book and hope you enjoyed it. I would be extremely grateful if you could leave a review on Amazon. I'd also love to hear your comments and am happy to answer any questions you may have, so do please get in touch with me by:

Email: roy.clark@royclarkauthor.com
Facebook: www.facebook.com/roy.clark.714
Facebook: www.facebook.com/mccannsfarmmayo
Website: www.royclarkauthor.com

If you enjoy reading memoirs, I recommend you pop over to Facebook group We Love Memoirs to chat with other authors and me. www.facebook.com/groups/welovememoirs

Acknowledgements

I'm sad to say that I've never kept a diary, so writing this memoir has been quite a challenge, and in some instances it would have been impossible if it weren't for my clear-thinking wife, Justi, who jogged my patchy memory on more than a few occasions.

So, firstly, I'd like to thank her, not only for her selfless help and encouragement in writing this book, but also for being my best friend and the person I've shared many of my life's adventures with.

My thanks to Justi's sister Cath and her husband, Vic, who have readily supplied advice and support over the years and have given us the thumbs-up for almost all our madcap ideas.

I'm indebted to the people of the Scottish Highlands and the Slovenes who welcomed us and with whom we still share lasting friendships.

I would, of course, also like to thank my publisher, Ant Press, and Victoria Twead who inspired me with her own series of memoirs. Last, but not least, thanks to my editor, Jacky Donovan, whose abundant help and utter professionalism whipped me into meeting my deadlines and giving my best shot.

Ant Press Books

If you enjoyed this book, you might also enjoy these Ant Press titles:

MEMOIRS

Chickens, Mules and Two Old Fools by Victoria Twead (Wall Street Journal Top 10 bestseller)

Two Old Fools ~ Olé! by Victoria Twead

Two Old Fools on a Camel by Victoria Twead (thrice New York Times bestseller)

Two Old Fools in Spain Again by Victoria Twead

Two Old Fools in Turmoil by Victoria Twead

Two Old Fools Down Under by Victoria Twead

One Young Fool in Dorset (The Prequel) by Victoria Twead

One Young Fool in South Africa (The Prequel) by Joe and Victoria Twead

Fat Dogs and French Estates ~ Part I by Beth Haslam

Fat Dogs and French Estates ~ Part II by Beth Haslam

Fat Dogs and French Estates ~ Part III by Beth Haslam

Fat Dogs and French Estates ~ Part IV by Beth Haslam

From Moulin Rouge to Gaudi's City by EJ Bauer

South to Barcelona: A New Life in Spain by Vernon Lacey

Simon Ships Out: How One Brave, Stray Cat Became a Worldwide Hero by Jacky Donovan

Smoky: How a Tiny Yorkshire Terrier Became a World War II American Army Hero, Therapy Dog and Hollywood Star by Jacky Donovan

Smart as a Whip: A Madcap Journey of Laughter, Love, Disasters and Triumphs by Jacky Donovan

Heartprints of Africa: A Family's Story of Faith, Love, Adventure, and Turmoil by Cinda Adams Brooks

How not to be a Soldier: My Antics in the British Army by Lorna McCann

Moment of Surrender: My Journey Through Prescription Drug Addiction to Hope and Renewal by Pj Laube

One of its Legs are Both the Same by Mike Cavanagh

A Pocket Full of Days, Part 1 by Mike Cavanagh

Horizon Fever by A E Filby

Horizon Fever 2 by A E Filby

Cane Confessions: The Lighter Side to Mobility by Amy L. Bovaird

Completely Cats - Stories with Cattitude by Beth Haslam and Zoe Marr

Fresh Eggs and Dog Beds: Living the Dream in Rural Ireland by Nick Albert

Fresh Eggs and Dog Beds 2: Still Living the Dream in Rural Ireland by Nick Albert

Fresh Eggs and Dog Beds 3: More Living the Dream in Rural Ireland by Nick Albert

Don't Do It Like This: How NOT to move to Spain by Joe Cawley, Victoria Twead and Alan Parks

Longing for Africa: Journeys Inspired by the Life of Jane Goodall. Part One: Ethiopia by Annie Schrank

Longing for Africa: Journeys Inspired by the Life of Jane Goodall. Part Two: Kenya by Annie Schrank

A Kiss Behind the Castanets: My Love Affair with Spain by Jean Roberts

Life Beyond the Castanets: My Love Affair with Spain by Jean Roberts (coming 2020)

FICTION

Parched by Andrew C Branham
A is for Abigail by Victoria Twead (Sixpenny Cross 1)
B is for Bella by Victoria Twead (Sixpenny Cross 2)
C is for the Captain by Victoria Twead (Sixpenny Cross 3)
D is for Dexter by Victoria Twead (Sixpenny Cross 4 (coming 2020))

NON FICTION

How to Write a Bestselling Memoir by Victoria Twead

CHILDREN'S BOOKS

Seacat Simon: The Little Cat Who Became a Big Hero by Jacky Donovan
Morgan and the Martians by Victoria Twead

Ant Press Online

Why not check out Ant Press's online presence and follow our social media accounts for news of forthcoming books and special offers?

Website: www.antpress.org
Facebook: www.facebook.com/AntPress
Instagram: www.instagram.com/publishwithantpress

Printed in Poland
by Amazon Fulfillment
Poland Sp. z o.o., Wrocław

54332178R00125